Self-Talk

The Ultimate Guide to Transforming Negative Thinking into Positive Thinking and Skyrocketing Self-Esteem, Confidence, Productivity, and Mental Toughness, Including 500 Daily Affirmations

© **Copyright 2019**

All Rights Reserved. No part of this book may be reproduced in any form without permission in writing from the author. Reviewers may quote brief passages in reviews.

Disclaimer: No part of this publication may be reproduced or transmitted in any form or by any means, mechanical or electronic, including photocopying or recording, or by any information storage and retrieval system, or transmitted by email without permission in writing from the publisher.

While all attempts have been made to verify the information provided in this publication, neither the author nor the publisher assumes any responsibility for errors, omissions or contrary interpretations of the subject matter herein.

This book is for entertainment purposes only. The views expressed are those of the author alone, and should not be taken as expert instruction or commands. The reader is responsible for his or her own actions.

Adherence to all applicable laws and regulations, including international, federal, state and local laws governing professional licensing, business practices, advertising and all other aspects of doing business in the US, Canada, UK or any other jurisdiction is the sole responsibility of the purchaser or reader.

Neither the author nor the publisher assumes any responsibility or liability whatsoever on the behalf of the purchaser or reader of these materials. Any perceived slight of any individual or organization is purely unintentional.

Contents

INTRODUCTION 1

CHAPTER 1: WHERE DOES NEGATIVE SELF-TALK COME FROM? ... 3

    THE POWER OF THOUGHT 4

    THE SUBCONSCIOUS MIND 5

    THE ORIGINS OF NEGATIVE THOUGHTS 6

    SO HOW DOES IT WORK? 8

    THE BLANK SLATE 10

    THE SELF-TALK JOURNAL 11

    WHEN SOMETHING BECOMES A PROGRAM, IT'S AN AUTOMATIC RESPONSE 12

    THE FORMATION OF HABITS AND DESIRES 13

    EXTERNAL CIRCUMSTANCES CREATE NEGATIVE THINKING: YOU HAVE TO
    CHANGE IT FROM WITHIN.. 14

    SIMPLE WAYS TO REPROGRAM YOUR THOUGHT PROCESSES AND FEELINGS 15

    CHANGING YOUR HABITS 15

    NEGATIVE EMOTIONS ARE NORMAL 17

    AFFIRMATIONS 18

    REPROGRAMMING THE SUBCONSCIOUS MIND 20

CHAPTER 2: WHY SELF-LOVE MATTERS 22
HOW AND WHY NEGATIVE SELF-TALK MANIFESTS IN NEGATIVE RESULTS 23
THE REALITY DISTORTION FIELD 25
LEARNED HELPLESSNESS 30
REFRAMING YOUR THOUGHTS 32
ADOPT AN ATTITUDE OF BEING IN CONTROL 33
CATEGORIZING YOUR NEGATIVE SELF-TALK 34
TURN NEGATIVE THOUGHTS INTO POSITIVE THOUGHTS 35
THE IMPORTANCE OF RAISING CHILDREN WITH A POSITIVE ATTITUDE 35

CHAPTER 3: THE LEVELS OF SELF-TALK 42
ACCEPTANCE AND HARMFUL SELF-TALK 42
RECOGNIZING NEGATIVE SELF-TALK AND THE NEED TO CHANGE IT 44
MAKING A DECISION TO CHANGE 47
CAN-DO SELF-TALK (BETTER YOU) 51
UNIVERSAL AFFIRMATION 52
SUMMARY: THE FIVE LEVELS OF SELF-TALK 53

CHAPTER 4: STOP THE BLAME GAME 54
BLAMING SOMEONE ELSE FOR YOUR PROBLEMS 55
BLAMING YOURSELF 59
MANIPULATIVE BLAME 61

CHAPTER 5: CONFRONTING NEGATIVE SELF TALK 63
RECOGNIZING NEGATIVE SELF-TALK 63
CATCHING YOURSELF USING NEGATIVE SELF-TALK 65
LABELING NEGATIVE SELF-TALK 66
TELLING YOUR NEGATIVE THOUGHTS TO F-OFF 66
CHANGING PERSPECTIVES 68
REPLACING NEGATIVE THOUGHTS 69
GETTING RID OF NEGATIVE SELF-TALK AND REPLACING IT CAN CHANGE HOW YOU FEEL 71

CHAPTER 6: FOSTERING SELF ESTEEM 73
- STOP BEING YOUR OWN BULLY 73
- RECOGNIZING YOURSELF AS WORTHY 74
- STEPS TO FOSTER SELF-LOVE AND SELF-ESTEEM 74
- TAKE UP HOBBIES OR VOLUNTEER 78
- BUILDING A FOUNDATION OF SELF-ESTEEM 79
- BECOMING A LEADER OF SELF 81

CHAPTER 7: EMOTIONAL INTELLIGENCE 83
- AWARENESS 83
- REGULATING YOUR EMOTIONS 85
- BECOMING SENSITIVE TO EMOTIONAL SIGNALS 86
- CHANGING YOUR EMOTIONAL STATES 86

CHAPTER 8: STRENGTHEN THE MENTAL MUSCLE 88
- GET TOUGH AND HAVE YOUR OWN BACK 88
- REMAINING STRONG IN THE FACE OF ADVERSITY 90
- TIPS FOR MAINTAINING A STRONG MINDSET AND STAYING POSITIVE 90

CHAPTER 9: 500 AFFIRMATIONS FOR A POSITIVE AND OPTIMISTIC OUTLOOK 92

CONCLUSION 112

CHECK OUT ANOTHER BOOK BY MARK DUDLEY 114

YOU MIGHT LIKE THIS ONE AS WELL 115

Introduction

All-day long, during every waking moment, our minds are chattering. We think to ourselves, plan out our day, and also criticize ourselves and express our deepest inner beliefs. This inner self-critic is the most devastating of all, worse than any shaming by other people—even though that hurts too. But it is our beliefs about ourselves that cut the deepest wounds.

The beliefs that you hold about your abilities, worth, future, and appearance, among other things, are woven deep into your subconscious. These beliefs can lead to destructive negative self-talk that holds you back from living the most fulfilling and happy life that you can lead. Negative self-talk and the destructive beliefs behind it create bad habits and lead to bad life choices.

That may sound depressing, and many people hold one specific belief that is as destructive as all the others combined—that they cannot change these core inner beliefs that lead to negative self-talk, negative attitudes, and the trap that they create for our lives.

However, we now know that this isn't the case—changing your core beliefs and negative self-talk is something that is in your reach today. And that's what we're going to teach you about in this book.

We will begin by discussing where negative self-talk and the core beliefs that lead to it come from. Then we'll explain the importance of self-love, and how to embrace it without becoming narcissistic. We'll talk about the importance of a positive attitude, and how to instill it in your children. Then we'll explore the process of recognizing your own negative beliefs and sore points, and how to turn them into strengths. From here, we'll teach you how to eliminate negative thoughts and self-talk, and replace them with a positive can-do attitude. We'll end the book with 500 affirmations that you can use to retrain your mind into a new optimistic, uplifting, and positive self that inspires.

Chapter 1: Where Does Negative Self-Talk Come From?

So, what is self-talk? It's the constant chatter that goes on in our minds. It reflects how we view ourselves and the world around us. You are probably only barely aware of it most of the time, even though it's having a large influence on your own thought patterns and results in life.

Most of the time, self-talk is that "voice in our head." Sometimes it is commenting on regrets from the past, dreams not realized, or mistakes made. Other times, it is talking about the future. Maybe it's telling you that you have dreams, but you aren't going to realize them. All too often, that voice in your head—the voice of your subconscious—is pointing out all of your shortcomings. That inner voice is all too happy to point out the reasons why you aren't going to succeed, or why you can't have a good relationship.

When you're by yourself at home or driving around in your car, the inner voice is probably speaking out loud. Don't worry about it; we all talk to ourselves. But we may differ in the ways that we talk to ourselves. For many of us, our self-talk is negative and brings us down.

Before we can go about changing the negative self-talk and thoughts that plague our lives, we need to understand where they come from in the first place. It turns out that our lives are in part directed by subconscious programs that have been instilled in us since childhood. This is the key to understanding how to change your life. Although we also have a core belief that those programs cannot be changed, just like a computer that can be reprogrammed, our subconscious mind can be reprogrammed as well. In order to do that properly, we need to begin by understanding how it operates in the first place and how those programs were created. This is the topic we are going to investigate in this first chapter.

The Power of Thought

The topic of the subconscious mind is a very large one, indeed. It crosses over many fields of study, including psychoanalysis, cognitive therapy, and neuroscience, among many others. But you don't need to know all the theories about cognitive therapy, or the fundamentals espoused by Carl Jung, in order to have a grasp of how the subconscious programming in your mind works and how to change it. You don't have to be an expert in neuroscience either. To be quite honest, it really doesn't matter how the brain is structured for our purposes.

We begin by making a simple observation about the world. Everything that human beings do or say begins as a thought. It doesn't matter how big or small the task before us is. Landing a man on the moon, or building the Brooklyn Bridge, began as mere thoughts in people's heads. The chair or sofa that you are sitting in as you read this book was also nothing more than a thought at one time. Thought can be said to be one of the main characteristics—if not the central characteristic—that separates humans from other life on earth. We not only have thoughts, but we are able to express them to others and influence the thoughts that others have. This ability to communicate our thoughts is also central to the human experience. Dogs and cats may have thoughts, but they have a limited ability to communicate them. The same holds true for other animals, and it is our ability to speak and communicate through the written word that has made the difference for human beings.

Thoughts not only shape what human beings can do in the world. They also shape how we view ourselves, our abilities, our appearance, and our relationships with others. Many of us have been trapped by negative thinking in regard to these fundamental thoughts that influence how we feel about ourselves. The impacts of this are wide and far-ranging. Even worse, most people are not even aware of how their negative self-talk is influencing their day-to-day lives and the outcomes that they experience.

So how is the power of negative thoughts—expressed through negative self-talk—realized in our life? If only we could count the ways. Some of the ways that negative self-talk expresses itself include bad or toxic relationships, failure to advance in a career, financial problems, and an inability to lose weight. Negative self-talk can also make us shy and afraid to express ourselves. We become plagued by self-doubt and lack confidence. In truth, the list that I provided right here is merely the beginning of the many things in your life that are influenced by negative self-talk. The negative core beliefs that you have about yourself are expressed daily through negative thoughts. Self-talk is directing the path of your life. But the good news is that you can change it starting right now.

The Subconscious Mind

In order to change the negative self-talk that has governed your life up to this point, you need to understand where it came from in the first place. In practice, it comes from the subconscious mind. The subconscious mind actually isn't as mysterious as it's made out to be. In fact, the subconscious mind is pretty dumb. I would equate the subconscious mind to a blank computer that only does what it's programmed to do. So, in order to change our core beliefs about ourselves, and to change our thought patterns, all we need to do is reprogram the subconscious.

Knowing how to reprogram the subconscious is the first step in moving forward and improving your life. But before we get to that, we need to understand where the negative programs came from in the first place.

The Origins of Negative Thoughts

I have a feeling that this part of the book won't be a surprise to anyone. The negative thoughts that you experience every single day are not real. They were programmed into your mind years—and even decades—ago. The subconscious mind begins the process of being programmed from the time that we are small infants. Anyone who interacted with you when you were a small child had a big influence on the negative thoughts that you are experiencing today. This begins with imparting a general attitude about life and the world and includes your basic view of yourself.

Obviously, your parents or immediate caregivers had a very large impact on shaping your thoughts. Think about how many parents tell their children things like, "You never do anything right!" Some parents even tell their children things like "You're stupid!" and "You're never going to amount to anything!"

But don't blame your parents. Remember that their minds were programmed too, and this has been going on for countless generations, stretching way back through the past. In many cases, parents don't even realize what they are doing or what kind of attitudes they are imparting to their children. If you had a parent like this, forgive them. They were struggling with the same type of inner negative self-talk that you are.

However, it should be straightforward to recognize that if you keep hearing "You're never going to amount to anything," then you are most likely going to adopt this viewpoint into your own life, and once this happens, you'll be the one saying it—in your own self-talk.

Your parents were not the only ones that were having a major influence in those crucial formative years. During ages 2-6, the subconscious mind is especially vulnerable. At this point, it's still a blank slate that is easily programmed. That makes it vulnerable to interactions with other people.

If you had older siblings, they could have a very dramatic impact on your subconscious programming. It's natural for siblings to be competitive, and when you have an older brother or sister, they might be going out of the way to put you down and instill negative thinking in your mind. Of course, I am not saying that all siblings have relationships like this, but it is quite common and even natural.

The same holds for relationships between children. Some of the cruelest people on the planet are children, who can be very mean to their peers between ages 6-17. The range of cruelties can be quite varied. They can push the idea that you are stupid, ugly, fat, uncoordinated—you name it. Perhaps the greatest cruelty of all is shunning.

In many tribal societies, shunning someone and forcing them to leave the group was one of the most dramatic actions that people could take. This even continued into the world of ancient civilization, where people were forced to move to remote islands, even during Roman times.

But this practice hasn't left us. One of the worst things that can happen to a child is they can live in a world where they have no friends because they have been shunned—in a manner that really isn't very different from what happened in many ancient societies. But unless your parents are able to move you into another school and situation, you're actually forced to live among the people who are rejecting you. This can have devastating and long-lasting impacts.

If your parents hire baby sitters or caregivers, they can also create negative thought-processes in your mind. Again, the baby sitter may not even be aware of what he or she is doing; their mind has also been programmed via the subconscious. But they can make negative statements about the children they care for, and given the fact that the subconscious mind is wide open for programming and easily influenced, any statements about you made by other adults or older children in your life while you were a small child can have a big influence.

Another big influence that is strongest when we are aged 5-10 but can still have an impact through the teen and early adult years, is the thoughts and opinions of teachers. Teachers that are positive and uplifting can have a big influence on a child and the thought patterns that the child has. But the opposite is equally true as well. If a teacher has a negative and abusive relationship with the children in their class, or with a specific child, the negative impact can last a lifetime. Think about the many beliefs that a teacher can impart to their students: *you can't do the math; girls don't study engineering; you're slow; you don't speak very well*. The list goes on, and it's a long one. Again, don't blame the teacher. They were programmed just like anyone else who imparted negative self-views on your life.

This brings us to an interesting psychological phenomenon called projection. When a person suffers from a given malady (usually of an emotional or mental nature), they will accuse others of suffering from it. You can think of people that have negative attitudes about others, especially small children, as engaging in the form of projection. The teacher or parent has a negative self-image, and they project this onto others around them.

Your negative self-programming can be influenced in other ways; sometimes these are indirect. If your parents had a toxic relationship, this could also lead to feelings of self-doubt and low self-esteem. You may have heard your father yelling at your mother telling her she was stupid, or maybe your mother called your father "a no-good bum." A small child hearing these types of interactions is ripe for incorporating these thought patterns into their own programming.

So How Does It Work?

The key to these types of thought patterns being adopted by the subconscious mind is repetition. The more the negative statement is heard, the more the subconscious mind incorporates it and learns it. If the statement is incorporated by strong emotions—then it becomes deeply ingrained in the subconscious. Of course, this is going to be the case if someone you love and admire, especially a respected adult, says negative things about you. A parent who is saying something negative will have the largest impact when you are a small child, but when you become school age and hear negative things from teachers or peers, the emotional impact can be just as strong.

When a message is repeated often, or it's accompanied by strong emotions, our subconscious mind accepts it readily. The ability of the subconscious mind to incorporate a message and use it in its programming is stronger when we are young, but it still has this capacity now.

That message won't just be reflected in our inner voice. The negative thoughts—*I'm stupid, I'm fat, I'm ugly, I can't do anything right*—turn into self-fulfilling prophecies. If you believe you're ugly, you'll avoid talking to that person that you're romantically interested in. Or if you do, your negative self-image will make you shy and awkward, ensuring that the result you expect—that they aren't going to be interested in you—is realized. For some people, over time this leads them to seek out toxic relationships, and they may find themselves stuck in an abusive situation, or in one that is constantly filled with lots of drama. Or maybe you avoid relationships altogether, thinking you're not good enough, and so you drift through life feeling lonely.

In fact, that is one path people with negative self-talk often take. The safe path, where safety is defined as the avoidance of situations that might lead to failure. As a result, you might find that you're leading a mediocre life, in the sense that you're not living up to your potential.

Stability is often elusive for people with negative self-talk. If you aren't involved in abusive relationships, you might find yourself having financial problems. When you sit back and take a look, you'll notice that you're never able to realize your goals. Maybe you can't seem to pay off your debts or you never lose weight. Or you're unable to hold a good job and find yourself bouncing from one place of employment to another, never advancing in your career.

Keep in mind that no one person is likely to experience all of these problems, so you might not see yourself in all of them. But one thing we can be sure of is this. If your mind is governed by negative thought patterns, and you are bombarded daily by your negative self-talk, it's holding you back in many ways. In the next section, we are going to go through an exercise so that you can start to become more consciously aware of your negative self-talk, and recognize the ways that it's holding back progress in your life.

The Blank Slate

When you are born, your subconscious mind is barely forming. It really starts to take root at around age two. When we become capable of language and verbal communication with others, our subconscious mind begins developing at a rapid pace, accepting the programming that is given to it.

I like to think of it as a new computer. When you buy a brand-new computer, it has a nearly empty hard disk that is ready to be filled up with information and programs. It runs at tip-top speed. But the more you use it, the more filled up the hard disk becomes, and that once impressive speed and performance becomes more elusive.

The same thing happens with our subconscious mind. As we get older, it's thoroughly programmed. The negative thoughts and self-talk that we experience are so ingrained that we are hardly aware of it, and it is having a real impact on our lives.

When you have a computer that's been used a lot and the hard drive is almost full, it takes some work to bring it back to peak performance again. The same is true of the subconscious mind. It can be reprogrammed. But it's going to take some work. That means you're going to have to put in a conscious effort on a daily basis to "reprogram" yourself. At first, it's going to seem like you're getting nowhere. It's not going to be easy replacing the negative thoughts and emotions that have been in place for decades. But if you stick with it, I promise you that it can be done. And the results are going to be breathtaking.

The Self-Talk Journal

The first step to solving any problem is to recognize it. With this in mind, I encourage you to get a notebook to use as a self-talk journal. This is an incredibly private thing, and it is up to you if you want to share it. If you want to keep it to yourself, that is perfectly fine as well.

The purpose of this exercise is to start becoming consciously aware of your negative self-talk. You probably have some conscious awareness of it, but we want to explicitly identify it.

There are two different ways that the journal can be organized. The straightforward way is to simply write down the negative thoughts that you have each day. Alternatively, you can create a group of categories. This could be done in a multi-subject notebook, for example. The categories could include things like appearance, weight, relationships, career, and intelligence. At first, you might not be sure what categories to use because you may not have been paying close attention to your negative thought patterns. When you become fully consciously aware of them for the first time, you will begin to notice where your negative self-talk is directed, and then you can pick the areas of your life that are most frequently impacted by these thoughts.

Either way, when you write down a negative thought or self-talk that you're experiencing, think about the opposite thought. You can write your thoughts in two columns, with the negative thought on the left side. Then write down the positive thought across from it on the right-hand side. Alternatively, you can simply list your negative thoughts linearly, and put the positive thought below it. For example, if the negative thought is "I always screw up," you can replace it with "We all make mistakes, and I will learn from my mistakes and do better next time." Another example: if you say "I'm stupid" to yourself, you could write down, "I am smart and capable" for your positive thought.

The point of this exercise is to become aware of the negative thoughts you are experiencing and to begin getting your mind to think in different ways that are positive and optimistic.

When Something Becomes a Program, It's an Automatic Response

The first step in the programming process is to condition your subconscious mind into believing something specific about yourself. It then acts back out on the world, in the form of responses to various situations. One of the responses is the negative self-talk that you continually experience. As a simple example, imagine a teenager seeing someone they are attracted to. If their life is governed by negative thoughts, the first thing that their inner voice might say is "They would never go out with me." This negative self-talk then results in practical consequences, namely not talking to the person and therefore getting the result imagined when thinking this way. A perfect example of a self-fulfilling prophecy.

One way that automatic responses are regulated is in your attitude. You can have an attitude of failure, and not even realize it. The negative self-talk that you experience is a result of your attitude, which in turn, like the self-talk that you experience, has been created by the programs that people have been putting into your life from day one.

A program that directs your subconscious mind and the resulting attitudes and self-talk that you experience every day, can also be influenced by something that happens in your adult life. One single off-hand negative comment can create a new negative program that begins operating in your subconscious. In fact, it's amazing how easily we accept negative statements by people and incorporate them into the programs that run our life. Someone might say something like "Those pants are too tight for you," and it will either create or reinforce a belief that we are overweight. As this new negative program is being created, you'll get that sinking feeling in your chest and stomach immediately when the person says it. Then it creates a negative thought such as *I'm fat,* and this is coupled with an attitude, such as *I can never lose weight.*

This brings us to another point to consider in your exercise with a negative self-talk journal. Look at the types of negative thoughts that your self-talk is describing to you. Think about them and then determine what kind of attitude they represent. Then commit to changing the attitude itself.

The Formation of Habits and Desires

The programming that has shaped your subconscious mind has created a set of automatic responses that we can also call habits. These habits are things that you may only be tangentially aware of—if you are aware of them at all. Maybe you are always late. You might always show up late to meet friends for dinner, or maybe you show up late to work or to meetings. There can be many causes of a habit like this, but if it's a result of negative thought patterns, which often produce depression and apathy, the results of your late behavior will only confirm what you already believe about yourself. Your friends might not invite you out as often, or you might get reprimands from your boss or even lose your job.

Desires are emotions that are at the root of our behaviors. Desire is the energy source for the actions we take in our lives. Positive desires can lead to positive results. For example, you might desire to move into a better neighborhood, but it's more expensive. If you are a person with a positive outlook on life, you'll devise a plan to realize your dream. Maybe you'll take on a second job, or work to get a promotion so that you can increase your salary.

The person whose life is dominated by negative self-talk has desires as well, but their negative self-talk works to dampen the desire so that it cannot provide the energy needed to make something happen. If your psyche is dominated by negative self-talk, when your desire springs to move to a better neighborhood, you'll talk yourself out of it. You'll tell yourself all the reasons why it's impossible. *I can't afford it. I could never afford it. I'll never make enough money to move over there.*

When a program has become deeply ingrained into our subconscious mind, it creates habits, which are a series of automatic behaviors in our lives. It's been said that these habits are like a plane running on autopilot. The plane just flies along and heads to its pre-determined destination. If you've been programmed into negative thinking, you're flying on autopilot, living a life governed by negative habits that prevent you from being completely happy and fulfilled.

External Circumstances Create Negative Thinking: You Have to Change it From Within

As we stated earlier, your subconscious mind was programmed by your early interactions and experiences. These highly formative experiences have become thoroughly ingrained by the time you hit adolescence, although your experiences in adolescence can also strongly shape your internal programs as well. If you have a good experience in your teenage years and early adulthood, it is possible to overcome negative programs and replace them with positive thinking. But for many of us, the negative programs are reinforced. Bad experiences in adolescence, which is a period of time characterized by extremely high levels of emotion, can strongly ingrain negative emotions and self-talk, essentially making them permanent unless we consciously work to invoke change.

That change has to come from within. You can't change by blaming your parents, your teachers, or childhood friends. You can't change by blaming bad experiences or outcomes. You have to take charge of your own life and the results that come with it. This is the meaning of "personal responsibility."

Simple Ways to Reprogram Your Thought Processes and Feelings

If you feel negative all the time, for most people, this is going to be reflected in their behavior. Some people are able to put a happy face over their negative self-image, but for most of us, it's going to carry forward into our behavior. A person that feels bad about themselves will often carry themselves in a negative way. They won't look people in the eye or smile. They may have a slouched posture. They will speak in a low voice, without enthusiasm. They'll feel tired all the time.

What if this person (maybe it is you) simply approached the world differently? The subconscious mind has been programmed, and it controls us if we let it do so. But you don't have to let it control you. Try walking out the door with an erect posture and a smile. Make an effort to look people in the eye, and speak with some enthusiasm.

Changing Your Habits

One of the first ways you can start eliminating negative self-talk is to change the habits that result from it. The first step is to identify all of your bad habits that arise from your negative attitudes, and the negative self-talk that results from those attitudes. At first, it is going to seem artificial, but you can make a lot of progress by forcing yourself to adopt habits that are associated with the opposite, positive attitude. Maybe you are late to work all the time because you have an attitude of failure. Sure, you can and should work on the attitude of failure, but something that will start to reverse it quickly at the subconscious level, is simply arriving to work early each day. Start acting as if you have the enthusiasm to go wherever you need to go so that you switch from being the person who is always ten minutes late to the person who is five minutes early.

The fact is that programs in our subconscious mind work in both directions. So, you can become conditioned to think a certain way, and then this thinking process and point of view becomes adopted by your subconscious mind. Then it acts outward, creating negative thought patterns and self-talk, and the negative habits and behaviors that come with it. For example, if you have a poverty mindset, the simple reality is that you are going to manifest a poverty cycle. You are going to hear constant mind chatter that only people who are connected and lucky make money, and you're never going to get out of the situation that you are in. Constantly hearing that kind of talk will put you in a trap, because you are going to act in ways that are consistent with the mindset. You won't be looking for any ways to get out of your current work situation, to improve your pay, upgrade your skillset, or start a business. Instead, you will find ways to cast blame on others and external circumstances.

But the good news is that we can go the other way, and reprogram our subconscious using our own active efforts. In your childhood, the programming of your subconscious was set by the impressions, thoughts, and words of others. It still is, to some extent, and a negative remark from a loved one or a colleague at work can reinforce the negative programs that are already operating in your psyche.

However, we can start "rewriting" these programs ourselves, by consciously saying thoughts that we want to manifest (affirmations) and by changing our habits using conscious effort.

Maybe in the mornings, you wake up depressed, not wanting to face another day. Your habit may be to sleep until the very last moment when you have to get up, and then slowly get ready to drag yourself to work.

Try something different over the next week. If the weather is good, get up 30 minutes early instead of sleeping in, and go outside for a brisk walk. Put a smile on your face and make it a point to enjoy the walk. If you encounter others along the way, smile and say hello in a friendly manner, and be open to stopping and chatting with them for a minute and making new friends.

Do this for an entire week, and I will tell you with absolute certainty that you are going to find that you feel a lot better about your life. This one simple act by itself might start changing some of that negative self-talk that you are experiencing day-in and day-out.

Think of other behaviors that you can change that are related to your negative programs. In order to do this, you need to write down a list of the major areas in your life where you are feeling the most negativity.

Do you have a large debt to pay off? A student loan or credit card bills? Unfortunately, too many of us do these days. Maybe you've only been making the minimum payments. It will be difficult for many people to do, but put a small amount of money aside each month in order to increase your payments. Even if it's just $20, it will help, but if you can put $50 or $100 aside, that is even better. That way, you are not going to just be paying the minimum and taking eons of time to pay off the bill. I assure you that the first time that you pay that extra $20, by changing your action through conscious effort, you are going to change the way you feel about your life instantly. You are literally going to feel a weight lifting off your shoulders the first time that extra payment is made.

You can start making small changes like this throughout your life and experience the positive results—but it's going to be important that you commit to the changes. When you do, you're going to find that by working inward, using the conscious mind to force changes in your behavior, that you are going to start seeing changes in the self-talk that has been causing you problems and holding you back.

Negative Emotions are Normal

Everyone has negative emotions from time to time, and the emotions we experience are not the problem. It's the way that we *respond* to the emotions that is the root of the problem.

Think about the negative emotions you would feel if you knocked over a glass vase, and it breaks. You could say to yourself "I can't do anything right," or you can clean up the mess and tell yourself "I'll be more careful next time." If you've broken the glass vase in someone else's home or at work, acknowledge the mistake and offer to pay for it, and move on.

Naturally, you are going to feel negative about breaking something, or doing something wrong, or saying something hurtful to a loved one. But you can choose to view the event as a learning experience and move on, or you can dwell on it and use negative self-talk to keep focusing on it and grow it into a large problem, that ends up damaging your self-esteem.

Negative self-talk can be viewed as *destructive* self-talk because it gets in the way of your goals and ambitions. This is different from constructive criticism, which acknowledges a mistake and then seeks to find a way to make something good come from the mistake. So, it doesn't get in the way of progress, it helps you get there.

Affirmations

Remember that a habit and an attitude—the programming of our subconscious mind—is created by repetition and/or strong emotions. The good news is that we can do the reverse. You can reprogram your subconscious mind by using affirmations. Other people were doing the programming when you were growing up. Now it's your turn to do the programming and direct your own outcomes. Affirmations will work best when combined with habit changes.

Remember, the subconscious mind is dumb. It's like a computer that just does what it's programmed to do. While it takes some time and effort, we can readjust the subconscious mind from the top down. So, we are going to put in an effort to reprogram the mind, and we can use affirmations to fill our mind with the positive thoughts that we want to have. So, in short, this is a way to reprogram the subconscious mind using statements that we *want* to believe. These are positive and uplifting statements that are known as "affirmations."

To get you started, we have included 500 affirmations at the end of the book. That is just for starters. If you need affirmations for a specific area of your life, you can look online to find more. But after reading some affirmations, it shouldn't be too difficult to come up with your own. You can even use your negative self-talk to come up with affirmations to replace it. Remember, I suggested that in your journal you write down the positive thought that is the opposite of the negative self-talk you are troubled by.

When using affirmations, the trick is a lot of repetition. Studies show that when you learn something, the way you learn it is by doing it over and over. When you were in school, this is how you passed your exams. I suspect that most people learn what they need to learn for an exam by repeating it in their head over and over again. This helps move the fact—or whatever you are trying to learn—into the memory banks of your brain, and into the realm of the subconscious. That way, it can be automatically recalled. Your brain literally changes its structure in order to encode the new information.

Just think about that last statement for a little bit. Your brain was actually structured as you were growing up by the negative ideas that people were feeding your mind. This is why the negative programs run so efficiently today. It is as if they changed the hardware *and* the software.

Repetition is one of the most effective ways to do this, but strong emotion can help drive it down with a single occurrence. This is another thing that has been demonstrated in many studies. People will often remember traumatic events very well because the force of the emotion etches it into memory. The same thing happens when someone makes a negative comment about you if you are already in a position of having negative thought processes. If they say something implying that you are not good enough, are incompetent, are fat, ugly, or whatever the case may be—the emotional response to the comment will ensure that the thought the other person is conveying gets incorporated into your subconscious mind.

It may be difficult to replicate that kind of emotional response, but we do have the power to implement a program of repetition.

The power of repetition isn't just reflected in studying. It shows what it can do when people learn a new skill. Think of a professional tennis player. If they had to think about all the steps they use to locate and hit a tennis ball coming at them at high speed, they wouldn't possibly be able to do it. The conscious mind simply isn't capable of analyzing the situation and directing your limbs and muscles to respond appropriately in a short enough amount of time.

The way that it is done is through the subconscious. By using repetition over the course of years—what we commonly call "practice" when considering the acquisition of the skill of some type—the movements required are driven into the subconscious mind where they become automatic programs, just like the programs that direct our negative self-talk.

Reprogramming the Subconscious Mind

When it comes to replacing negative self-talk with positive thoughts, the way to start getting this done is to engage in the repetition of positive affirmations three times a day or more. You should keep the number of affirmations to a minimum. Start off by identifying an area of your life that you want to work on first. Then pick out three to five affirmations related to this topic and repeatedly say the affirmations to yourself during three daily meditation sessions. You should repeat each affirmation about five times per session. Say them slowly and methodically so that you aren't rushing through it.

At first, you aren't going to believe what you are saying. But as we've said before, the subconscious mind is a dumb receptacle. So, if you keep telling it what you want to believe, the subconscious mind is going to accept it, and incorporate the statements into its own programs. Once this happens, you will start to see your negative self-talk begin to change. If you combine this process with the use of habits, the changes you see will happen more rapidly and will be stronger.

Chapter 2: Why Self-Love Matters

Self-love is not about narcissism. We are talking about a perfectly normal level of self-esteem. But why is this important? I'm sure that you realize that with good self-esteem, you would feel better about yourself. But it goes way beyond that. Replacing the negative self-talk that you constantly experience with healthy and positive thoughts will actually change the direction of your life. You probably don't realize it, but the negative self-talk that you experience is actually holding back your potential for success. This cuts across all aspects of life. In other words, negative self-talk not only prevents you from having career success, but it will also inhibit your ability to get ahead financially. It's either going to prevent you from getting in relationships or ensure that you are trapped in bad and abusive relationships. Of course, I'm not saying this is going to happen to everyone, but on some level we are all affected by negative self-talk, which plagues our lives and sets limits on what we can do.

The reason is that negative self-talk creates a reinforcement mechanism that solidifies the negative beliefs that we have about ourselves. Those negative beliefs constrain the actions that we take in the real world. They also conspire to attract negative things into our lives. When you give negative thoughts energy, you are going to attract negative energy in return. This negative energy can take many forms. It might be in the form of bad people that are coming into your life. Or it might be in the form of bad outcomes and results. This is why self-love matters. Self-love is going to enable you to direct positive energy, instead of negative energy. And what that's going to do for you, besides making you feel better, is you are going to start seeing better results in your life.

How and Why Negative Self-Talk Manifests in Negative Results

Most of us aren't even fully conscious of the negative self-talk that we are experiencing every single day. And so, it's not surprising that we fail to make the connection between negative self-talk and the results this brings to our lives. In fact, we use it to justify the negative thoughts that continually run through our brains. Many people misinterpret the thoughts that they are experiencing, believing that they reflect the outcomes in their life, rather than the other way around. Now this isn't to say that you will never have a negative experience that leads to negative thought processes. That certainly does happen at times. But for those of us who are living a life that is dominated by negative self-talk, it's actually the other way around.

 So, what happens is: a negative experience or comment creates a belief system that leads to negative thoughts. The negative thoughts impact our actions in the present-day. This could have long-lasting implications. Suppose that you were a 12-year-old girl with an interest in mathematics and science. If the teacher that you looked up to came and told you that as a girl you could not do mathematics, that could cause a lot of self-doubts. Maybe the teacher is a little bit coy about their belief, so they don't come out and say it exactly like that. In fact, if they did, it might cause you to get angry at them and become determined to overcome the prejudice against you. So, what if instead they just simply told you that you didn't have the acumen required for a career in math and science? That is more likely to be incorporated into your psyche as a negative belief system. And this will have a direct impact on the future course of your life. After you come to believe that you are not good at math, you will then probably avoid taking more math and science courses in your schooling. And as a result, you will end up pursuing a totally different career path than you otherwise would have.

There are many other ways that negative comments can have an impact that goes well beyond simple negative thoughts. If someone is led to believe that they're ugly or undesirable as a partner, their heads will be full of negative thoughts about this on a daily basis. The negative thoughts will lead to depression and withdrawal. This can manifest in many ways, including shyness or an inability to speak clearly, which will actually confirm the perception. In other words, if you start acting shy and awkward, then people are not going to want to socialize with you. You will see the belief that you're not suitable as a romantic partner confirmed in the external world, and this will only strengthen the programs that are going on inside your mind.

So that is one example of what we might classify as a "self-fulfilling prophecy." There are many others. If you are young and have a perception that you're overweight, there is a good chance that you're going to end up as overweight later on in adulthood. Another self-fulfilling prophecy that is very common as a result of negative thought processes is financial troubles. People who have negative feelings about money or have a negative view about their ability to earn money, often find themselves later on in a state of just getting by—if not in outright poverty.

Negative self-talk also has an unfortunate effect on your health. Think about it. If you have negative emotions about many aspects of your life—if not all aspects of your life—that is going to heighten the stress and anxiety that you feel every single day. This is going to cause many physical symptoms, and the problem with the symptoms is that they are going to be general and vague. Many people will attribute them to working too much or simply due to aging. So, for example, you are probably going to suffer from a bit of insomnia. You might also experience a lot of body pains. It won't surprise you to learn that many people that suffer from negative thought processes and negative self-talk tend to be hypochondriacs. The constant stress and anxiety that is experienced can lead to symptoms such as chest pain or stomach pain. In fact, in some cases, the perceptions of pain can actually manifest as a real illness. If the person is lucky, they will only have headaches and possibly a stomach ulcer. While recent research has linked stomach ulcers to a type of bacteria, it still remains true that if you are under constant stress, and your life is filled with anxiety, that you are more likely to get a stomach ulcer.

Negative self-talk can cause many other health problems. It's possible to experience digestive problems such as diarrhea and to suffer from muscle tension and pain. In a worst-case scenario, the increased levels of stress combined with the lack of sleep can lead to an increased rate of illnesses.

Sadly, these problems seem to be only getting worse. The reason is that the rapid development of technology is causing some people to become more isolated. Social isolation can often make the problem worse. If you become withdrawn and have less social contact, that gives more time for your mind to fill itself with negative thoughts. This can further deepen the problem. If you are someone who has negative thought processes about your social worth, and then you're sitting at home having more thoughts and self-talk related to this topic, it might make you far less likely to venture out and make new friends.

The Reality Distortion Field

Someone once said that Steve Jobs created a reality distortion field. This was a comment made in relation to the way people became fanatical about Apple products. If your mind is filled with negative self-talk, you are creating your own reality distortion field. But unlike the reality distortion field associated with Apple products, the reality distortion field created by negative self-talk is going to be uniformly negative. This can lead to further perception problems and even serious mental health problems like depression. It's certainly going to lead to increased anxiety, especially in social situations.

When you are suffering from the reality distortion field created by negative thought processes, something that's going to happen is you're going to blow things way out of proportion. This can create conflict with people around you. At work, you might be known as someone who is "touchy." The negative thought processes that you continually experience are going to cause your self-esteem to plummet. And so, if anyone makes an offhand remark, you are more likely than the average person to interpret it in a negative way. Unfortunately, this is often going to happen even when the remark is objectively not negative. So, other people are going to start feeling guarded around you. This creates a snowball effect that leads to more negative thoughts in your mind, and the external reality created by your misperception only confirms the negative thoughts, like a self-reinforcement mechanism.

Another side effect caused by this negative reality distortion field is that you're going to be constantly playing the blame game. This can happen on two levels. First off, since you have a negative attitude about yourself, you are going to be blaming yourself for many of the actions that happen in your life. But in this case, we are talking about blaming yourself when you were not at fault. However, sometimes, you are also going to be blaming other people for your problems. And in this situation, the reality is that in fact you are the cause of the problems. We will talk about the blame game in a later chapter in more detail.

The reality distortion field caused by negative thought processes and self-talk often manifests itself in a belief system where your mind always seems to involve you in everything. The fact is, many things happen that seem to be directly connected to us, and sometimes people take actions that appear negative, but they really have nothing to do with us at all. But if you are trapped in the world of negative self-talk, you are more likely than not to interpret nearly every action and reaction in personal terms. Maybe someday a colleague shows up to work in a bad mood because she had a fight with her husband, and when you pass her in the hallway she isn't very enthusiastic about seeing you. Somebody with a healthy attitude might recognize that maybe she was having a bad day, and that's how they would interpret the interaction. But if you are trapped in a world of negative thought processes, you interpret everything in terms of you. So, in the same interaction, you would take it personally if the woman was not very friendly as she passed. You would be wondering what you did to upset her. Or even worse, you might use it as an excuse to reinforce your belief that you're not a worthy person.

Another impact of the reality distortion field created by negative thought processes is that people who have this problem will extend their negative beliefs to all aspects of life. For example, let's say that you are playing basketball with some friends, and you keep messing up, so your teammates get that little bit upset. Of course, from an objective perspective, most people will recognize that such events have very little significance. Once the game is over, your friends will completely forget what happened and move on. But if you're suffering from low self-esteem caused by negative self-talk, it's going to stick with you and you are going to use it as an example that supposedly illustrates your worth as a person in general. The incident will reinforce your negative beliefs about yourself and probably enhance depressive feelings.

Another very common way of negatively interpreting the world is known by psychologists as filtering. In any given situation, there are usually positive and negative things that happen. In order to objectively evaluate the situation, you would weigh the good and the bad and take the average. But if your life has been programmed so much that you're dominated by negative thought processes all the time, you filter out any positive things that happened. In fact, you may be filtering all day long, which means that every day, you will only see the negative aspects of what happened. When you only see the negative aspects of the events that happen in your life, it reinforces the negative views that you already had. And so, it will strengthen the negative self-talk that you are experiencing. Also, it's important to note that failing to see the good side of every event that happens will lead you to experience more negative results in the future.

Another problem that people have is called polarized or black-and-white thinking. In this case, you look at every action that you take in black-and-white terms. So, in other words, you are either perfect or are you are a failure. The problem with this is that striving for perfection is something that's virtually impossible. And since you cannot be perfect in every interaction, this will translate into viewing everything as a complete failure. Of course, most things that happened in life are not either perfection or failure. They are usually somewhere in the middle, and maybe weighted a little bit one way or the other. But by seeing everything as a failure, this only serves to reinforce the negative thought processes that are causing you to think this way in the first place. So almost every event that you experience is going to confirm the perception that you're not quite adequate, leading you to feel even more low self-esteem.

Another problem that often comes out of the reality distortion field of negative thought processes is what's called the control fallacy. This can manifest in one of two ways. The first way this can manifest is in a false belief that you have more control over outcomes and the way people behave than you actually do. Since people are often going to act in ways that you don't like, it's going to give the illusion that you are causing a lot of negative events when in reality you have nothing to do with it.

When it comes to people with negative thought processes, however, there is a more common way that the control fallacy manifests. This is in the belief that you have no control whatsoever over your life. That is, you believe that everything is working against you or everything is due to luck. You begin to see yourself as a victim in life. Someone who sees themselves as a victim is someone who's not going to take control of their life and institute changes that would be beneficial.

So, I want to take a step back at this time and congratulate you on reading this book. By reading this book, you are actually taking action. It may only be the first step on your journey, but taking that first step is a very important way to move forward. Simply by becoming more informed, you are getting away from the victim mentality.

Now, let's move onto another common thought process that is often found among people with negative self-talk. This is using the word "should," and the phrase "should have" far too often. Now, all of us have a list of things that we "should" do in order to improve ourselves. But if you start finding yourself with a big self-improvement "should" list, that can be an indication that you have a reality distortion field that isn't healthy. Perhaps the worst manifestation of this is living in the past and filling your thought processes with "should have." It's normal to have regrets. But it's not normal to continually live in the past. Yes, we all have things that we should have done in the past. But if you are continually focused on it, that indicates you need to take a step back. Learn your lessons from the past without dwelling on them.

Finally, we will end this section with one more aspect of distorted thinking that psychologists have focused on. This is called global labeling. We all fail at some task or in a relationship at some point. But what happens when a person is suffering from global labeling is that they generalize their failure in order to characterize their entire personality. The characteristic phrase associated with this outlook is "I'm such a loser." So, if the person makes a mistake—no matter how minor—they start feeling bad about themselves. But instead of just learning from the mistake and moving on, they generalize the feeling from the mistake into a general sense of low self-esteem and unworthiness.

Learned Helplessness

One of the main impacts of negative self-talk is creating boundaries for ourselves. As we have mentioned, this negative programming usually results from the negative thought processes that others have put into our subconscious minds over the years—stretching way back into our childhoods. This relates to a concept called self-efficacy, which is your ability to achieve goals.

When you are suffering from learned helplessness, you have a low amount of self-efficacy because you put up artificial obstacles subconsciously. This happens because you perceive a lack of control over your life.

Let's use the negative statement "I'm so stupid" as an example. Often, misguided parents will tell their kids they are stupid when they make a mistake. They don't do it because they really believe their children are stupid (at least most of the time). They have a misguided belief that by calling their children stupid, or pointing out that they are acting stupid in a given situation, they are going to motivate the child into behaving better in the future. Instead, what happens is the child incorporates the dysfunctional belief that they are stupid. Over the years, this will be reinforced.

It will start to set limits in the real world as well. If you start believing that you are stupid on a subconscious level, you are going to start feeling as though taking action, in some ways, is futile. So, you won't study as hard in school as you would have otherwise. As a result, you get mediocre grades—confirming the perception that you are in fact, stupid.

You will also fail to take action. Maybe by the time you go to work, the belief is thoroughly ingrained in your psyche. So, if you believe that your opinion and insights are not going to be valued, then you might doubt the value of them yourself. In meetings at work, you may remain quiet and aloof, and this might create a perception among others that in fact, you're not very capable. Doing the minimum to get by, since you have a total lack of belief in yourself, you might feel as though you can do no more. This will relegate you to the bottom rungs, and you'll never improve your situation.

This is an example of how learned helplessness can manifest many years down the road. This is but one example of a poverty mentality. People can have a poverty mentality for many different reasons, but in all cases, the poverty mentality is something that is going to hold people back from living up to their fullest potential. The poverty mentality is characterized by many of the distorted thought processes discussed in the last section. For example, if you have a poverty mentality, one thing you are going to do is blame others for your situation. You will also suffer from a mentality dominated by the control fallacy, believing that others (or "luck") are controlling your fate, rather than facing the reality that you control your own fate.

When you believe that you have no control over the situations that you find yourself in, then you are not going to take any action to get out of them. Your overall productivity and growth will suffer as a result. You are going to go through your life feeling resentful and bitter.

So how do you overcome learned helplessness? The first thing is to identify the limiting beliefs that are showing up in your life as a result of your negative thought processes. This is going to include many of the problems that we discussed in the previous section.

Start by looking at a negative experience after it happens and see how you attribute the cause. For example, you might make a mistake at work that leads to your boss reprimanding you. You might respond in this way:

"I am not good at anything I do."

But maybe there are other causes that led to the problem. Take a look at the situation and see if there are other explanations. Maybe you didn't sleep well the night before, or maybe a co-w0rker gave you incorrect information. The details of what you observe about the situation are less important than avoiding generalizing. This is one of the most insidious problems that arises from negative self-talk. Look at the statement above—it's generalized a minor mishap at work into something that describes your overall capabilities and worth as a person.

So, start by limiting negative events to the situation at hand. Sometimes we just have to accept that we made a mistake, but we also need to recognize that we can learn from the mistake and do better next time. And more importantly, we need to recognize that one mistake doesn't mean that we are a bad person in general.

One of the most negative thought processes that can arise from learned helplessness is a belief that you can't change. If you are experiencing learned helplessness, there is no doubt that this belief is manifesting itself in many negative thought patterns and self-talk that is ruling your daily life. It can be said to be a feeling that you are trapped by your negative situation. This is the victim mentality that many people are trapped in today. You can start improving your life very rapidly by dropping the victim mentality and thinking in terms of someone who is in control of their life. The first step in that journey is to reframe your thoughts.

Reframing Your Thoughts

One of the central ways that you can overcome negative self-talk is by reframing your thoughts. This requires you to do a little bit of analysis and turn your negatives into positives. One way is to use the ABCDE method that was developed by psychologist Martin Seligman, who was inspired by the ABC Model first developed by Albert Ellis. We are going to describe our own version of it.

The ABCDE method can be framed in the following way:

- A is for Adversity. We all experience adversity in our lives. The first step is to describe the adverse situation that happened, which led you to have negative thoughts about yourself.

- B is for Beliefs. Look for the beliefs that are determining how you have interpreted the event. When you start using these exercises, these will be the automatic beliefs that you have created in your subconscious mind as a result of years of negative programming.
- C is for Consequences. What are the consequences of your negative beliefs? In particular, look for the feelings you experience and also actions that you take, as a result of the beliefs that you connect to the adverse event.
- D is for Dispute. That is, look at any of the beliefs that you have connected to the situation and dispute those that are not objectively valid. Replace your inappropriate interpretations and actions that result from the event with better feelings and actions.
- E is for Energy. Focus on the feelings that you get by responding to the situation in a positive and appropriate way.

Adopt an Attitude of Being in Control

Of course, fate does play some role in our lives. You could have been born in poverty on some remote island. But you weren't, and we have to deal with the here and now and not hypotheticals. The fact is this: you have a lot of control over your own life and your fate. Start taking an attitude of control and watch your life improve as a result.

Being in control doesn't necessarily mean that you are going to be able to control the outcome of every situation, or that you can control what comes in and out of your life. What you definitely have control over is the way that you react to different situations. So, you can start there.

Second, although we can't control everything, the fact is that we actually do have a huge amount of control over major aspects of our lives. That doesn't mean we have complete control. Is everyone going to get into Harvard University? Of course not. But you can still get a good college education, and if you study hard, you will come out as educated as someone from Harvard and you will do just as well in the workplace.

Try setting some small goals and working to realize them. Achieving small goals is one way to start building self-confidence. When you start to see that you are able to set goals and achieve them, then you will start feeling more like you are in control of your own life. You will also begin to experience more positive self-talk in response to the increased levels of self-confidence, and your belief systems will begin to change.

Categorizing Your Negative Self-Talk

In the first chapter, we suggested that you keep a self-talk journal. Now that you have become aware of learned helplessness and the many different ways that your thought patterns can be dysfunctional in the reality distortion field, go back and take a closer look at your negative self-talk. See if you can categorize each of your thoughts in a particular manner. For example, is a thought representing black and white thinking? Or are you engaging in filtering? Sometimes a thought is going to fit more than one category, but you can try to list them as best you can. If a particular thought fits more in one category than another, then classify it with the one that best describes it. You can also count the number of times that you are having thoughts of a specific type and then add them up to see what percentage is the largest among the many possibilities.

This will help you understand your negative thought processes more clearly, and possibly help you to identify which characteristics of the reality distortion field best describe your overall thought process. For example, some people are going to find that they are suffering from black & white thinking. This will help them to develop an effective strategy to overcome their negative self-talk.

Turn Negative Thoughts into Positive Thoughts

Earlier, you wrote down a positive thought that was the opposite of a negative thought in your journal. Start doing this on an active basis. This is going to require developing your ability to recognize negative self-talk as it happens.

There are four key phrases that are associated with negative self-talk in terms of reality distortion and learned helplessness. These are:

- "I always …"
- "I can't …"
- "I never …"
- "I am …"

These phrases describe absolute statements. It is important to pick up when they appear in your inner dialogue and then actively replace them with a more appropriate thought.

For example, you can replace: "I never do anything right," with "I made a mistake in this situation, but I will do better next time." If you can start identifying and correcting statements that occur in your inner chatter, which involve these types of absolute qualifiers, you will go a long way to improving your negative self-talk.

The Importance of Raising Children with a Positive Attitude

As you can see from what we are discussing so far, it's going to be a difficult road to recovery once you've been trapped by the negative thought processes that plague many people's lives, especially when you reach adulthood. This is why it's important to raise children that have a positive self-image.

Of course, there is always a danger of creating a little narcissist. So, the goal should be to have children that have positive feelings of self-esteem, but not inflated views of themselves or their abilities. Sadly, there has been a little too much of the latter going around in recent decades. We certainly want children to feel good about themselves and to believe that they can achieve their goals if they set their minds to them, but not everyone is going to "save the world." So, it is important to have your children learn positive thought patterns that are realistic.

We certainly don't want to have children that adopt an attitude of learned helplessness. Your children are not victims, so make sure that they don't fall into that trap. When you spot your children adopting an attitude of learned helplessness, you can step them through the ABCDE method, so that they can learn to identify feelings of learned helplessness themselves and then work their way through the thought processes that are behind it and overcome them.

Second, since you are aware of the patterns of negative thinking that manifest in ways such as black and white thinking, generalization, and so forth, learn to recognize these destructive thought patterns in your children and then help them to get a more realistic picture of reality. So, if your child generalizes—that is, they make a mistake and then generalize it by thinking that as a result they are a "total loser" or "stupid"—help them to differentiate between the single act itself and their worth as an individual.

By starting to foster positive thinking while they are young, you can help your children build up a reserve of resilience. All of us are going to experience adversity throughout our lives, which is going to cause us to doubt ourselves. But if we have a strong foundation to lean on, then we won't give in to negative thought processes and then suffer the wide-reaching consequences of these.

If you are reading this book and suffering from negative self-talk yourself, you may have unconsciously imparted some of those thought patterns to your children. In fact, this has been going on for time immemorial, and it's the reason that these types of thought patterns are here now. They didn't materialize out of thin air, and you may have gotten your own negative self-talk from programs your own parents instilled in you during your childhood.

So now is your chance to break the cycle. Remember that you are not going to be the only influence in your child's life, and there are going to be some things that you cannot control. The only thing you can do is build a foundation for your child that they can call upon when confronted by negativity from teachers or peers. If you have more than one child, you can help the situation because many of us also get a lot of negative thought patterns and beliefs about ourselves from interactions with our siblings.

Simply getting rid of or preventing the victim mentality can go a long way to ensuring the success of your child as they grow up. So many people in today's world are held back as a result of this outlook.

There are some simple, practical steps you can take to help your children develop a habit of positive self-talk. Develop shortlists of affirmations for them to say. You can also help your children come up with their own positive affirmations.

Teach your children about the benefits of positive self-talk, and explain the problems with negative self-talk. As your children get older, these discussions can become more in-depth. You can also explain to them how to change a negative thought into a positive thought. Use specific examples that are directly relevant to their lives.

One important thought pattern that you want to get out of your child's mind is the belief that things happen because of luck. This type of thought needs to be replaced by the recognition that things happen as a result of the actions we take in our lives beforehand. So, if a child scores high on an exam, is that due to luck? Some children may think so, but the reality is that scoring high on an exam is due to studying hard in 99/100 cases. So, you might ask your child why they did good on an exam and have them explain in detail, and if they answer that it was due to "luck," you can offer them guidance in order to reframe this thought.

As another example, a child may have been rejected by a crush. You can help them to see that this is an isolated situation and that being rejected by someone they are attracted to does not generalize into negative subjective statements—such as that they are "ugly" or "undesirable." Help them to understand that there may be specific reasons for the rejection that might not even have anything to do with them, such as the love interest already being involved with someone else.

For smaller children, you can help them learn the power of positive thinking by making crafts that have positive thoughts on them. They can use these before going to school to start their day with a positive mindset.

Getting nervous in challenging, difficult, and new situations is one of the greatest difficulties that children will face. You can help them overcome this by teaching them positive thoughts to say to themselves when they recognize that they feel nervous.

You will also want to teach your children to avoid thinking in terms of regret. Imagine the lifetime of pain that they will avoid if they learn this skill early on. Teach them that the way to approach major mistakes that they made in the past is to learn what the mistake was, and avoid making it again in the future. Teach them that they should not dwell on past mistakes and keep replaying them in their heads.

You should also teach your children to recognize the absolutes that characterize negative thinking. If you remember, these included the phrases, "I never ...", "I am ...", "I can't ...", and "I always ...." Whenever a child uses these phrases in their language, this is something that should be addressed right away. These types of absolute statements characterize the type of thinking that we discussed in the "reality distortion field" section. Examine each statement of this type and then correct it, or should I say correct the misperception that is present in the statement.

For example, any absolute statement like "I never ..." should be easily replaced by a positive thought process. We all know that the world is not framed in absolute terms. But even us adults who are trapped by negative self-talk and negative thought processes often engage in these types of statements without realizing how unrealistic they are. So, one thing that's important to take care of is yourself. Before you get your children on a correct path to thinking positive thoughts, it's important that you are able to think in a correct manner first.

Another thing you need to instill in your children is how to recognize the context of a situation. For example, help them to recognize that people often say bad things that they don't really mean. A child may say a nasty comment to another child when they're upset about something else; and in fact, you probably realize that this can happen among adults as well. So, you should develop this skill on your own, and that will make it easier to teach your children how to interpret their interactions with others properly. Think back to the earlier example of someone who appeared unfriendly when greeting you at work. Remember it was suggested that maybe that person was having problems at home? The same thing may be influencing a situation involving your child. A peer on a sports team or at school could be having a bad day for some reason or another. Maybe they have problems at home, or a girl they are interested in rejected them, or they had a bad result on an exam. And so, they take this out on your child. Maybe you can discuss this with your child and ask them if they know of anything that might have happened to the other child to cause them to act in a negative way. The key point of this exercise is for your child to recognize that not everything is about them. Some people will react in a negative manner when the root cause is completely unrelated to you, and so you should not take the events as a reason to generate more negative thoughts about yourself.

Another thing that's important to deal with when it comes to children, is helping them to recognize that there is always another day. Children live more in the here and now than adults do. As a result of this, they are more likely to take an individual result or event far more seriously. In the heat of the moment, children may find it difficult to realize that there are going to be many more opportunities to redo the situation. For example, if they are an athlete, it may be hard for them to conceptualize the fact that they are going to have many seasons and games ahead of them, within which they can strive to perform far better than they did during the current game or practice that is causing them angst. So, part of your job as a parent is to help them recognize that today's game is not going to be the end of their story. It's just one event among many throughout their lives.

You can also take any negative situation and get the child to refocus. That is, help them to recognize the positives that occurred in this situation. If you remember when we discussed the reality distortion field, one of the dysfunctional methods of thinking that people who are trapped by negative self-talk engage in, is looking at things in a black-and-white fashion. Children are more likely than adults to look at situations in black-and-white terms. One of the things you can do, is to help them see that there are never situations that are entirely black-and-white. As part of this exercise, you can help them to recognize that the experience that they are currently seeing in black-and-white terms is actually full of shades of gray. That way, they can learn to pick out the positives from any situation and start learning to focus on those instead.

And of course, you need to help your child to learn that they are not a bad person or a failure if they recognize that they have made a mistake. Instead, the goal should be for them to recognize their mistakes, learn from their mistakes, and then move on. You can also get them to recognize that they should not only learn from their mistakes but they should take action to remedy the problems that led to the mistakes. So, if they scored badly on an exam, that might mean spending the next hour studying. If they played poorly in a basketball game, it could mean spending more time practicing their jump shot. We don't want to get into a situation where high self-esteem means that we never admit failure. The purpose of having positive self-esteem is to recognize that our mistakes don't define us as a person. However, we also need to recognize that we should take action to improve our performance in the future.

One way that you can approach this with children is to help them convert their absolute statements into a remedy that turns the statement into a more positive outlook. So, you should not discourage them from recognizing their mistakes. Instead, you want to teach them to pair their mistakes with a solution to the mistake. So instead of saying "I never do good on math exams," you can have them say something to the effect of: "That exam didn't go as well as I hoped, but I am going to practice doing long division until I learn to do it right."

One question that is often raised when it comes to dealing with these situations with children is the following—people want to know if they have to be perfect in their outlook themselves, before they can help their children develop positive thought patterns. The answer to this question is: absolutely not. In fact, helping your children to develop more positive thought patterns is going to be an active exercise that will help you to develop more positive thought patterns yourself. So it can actually be a very healthy way for you to engage and help your own situation, while simultaneously helping your child to develop the power of positive thinking.

Chapter 3: The Levels of Self-Talk

As you develop and begin to combat the self-talk that has been holding you back in your life, there are going to be different levels of progress or actually different levels of your self-talk. In this chapter, we are going to go over the levels of self-talk that are generally accepted by psychologists.

Acceptance and Harmful Self-Talk

The type of self-talk at this level is uniformly negative. It's characterized by phrases such as "I am ..." followed by a negative statement. Common examples have already been discussed, but let's reproduce a few here:

I am ugly.

I am a total loser.

I am fat.

Statements that also indicate an inability to act also fall in this category. If you can't act to change something, that makes you a helpless victim, so these types of statements are common among people who have learned helplessness. The assertion that you are unable to act might be paired with an excuse of some kind. Examples could be:

I can't get into college because I'm stupid.

I can't earn enough money, because I didn't go to college.

I can't stick to any diet.

I can't lose weight; I have a thyroid problem.

Of course, having a thyroid problem and not having gone to college can be real problems that hold people back, but these are problems that can be rectified. The key point here is the *attitude* that underlies the statement. That attitude is one of defeatism and creates situations in our minds that cannot be overcome. Therefore, these are not only self-limiting statements, but they are also statements that justify the negative behaviors that are keeping us from moving forward.

Another common phrase that is used in harmful self-talk is: "If only …."

If only I was taller, girls would go out with me.

If only I was born rich, I could live in a nice neighborhood.

Self-talk statements that include the phrase "if only" are excuses for the situation you might be in. At the subconscious level, this works to reinforce limiting behaviors, and then the end results you experience are justified in your mind. Another form of this type of thinking is to use the statement "I wish …."

I wish I was smart, and then I could go to a good university.

I wish I was rich, and then I could get a new car.

Focus on the mentality that underlies the statements. The type of mentality expressed here is one that avoids taking action to change circumstances, and it also has an implied suggestion that your current situation is justified. For example, maybe you have an old beat-up car that is constantly breaking down. Rather than reacting by improving your credit score to get a loan or working more hours to get enough money to buy a new car, you justify the situation and put the desired goal in an unattainable spot.

When you engage in self-talk like this, the subconscious accepts these phrases as directions or programmed statements, and then it will generate destructive behaviors that act in a manner of self-fulfilling prophecy.

At the very beginning of this process, you are going to be at the level of "acceptance." So, in other words, this means that you actually believe and accept your negative self-talk. This is the level of self-talk that most of us are at when we seek help for the first time. So, all those negative statements that you're making to yourself, or—to be clear—that your subconscious is making about you, your conscious mind hears them and believes them to be true as well.

Recognizing Negative Self-Talk and the Need to Change It

If you are reading this book, then chances are you have already moved past the acceptance stage. That's because you have recognized that you have a negative self-talk problem. However, this doesn't mean that you have solved the situation.

Sometimes people that are in this stage are engaging in a lot of self-talk that expresses a desire for change but without actually taking any action on that change. So, in the acceptance stage—to use an example—you might be focused on telling yourself "I am fat." Whether or not that statement has some objective truth to it is not really our concern at the moment, we are simply noting that you are having the thought. If you have moved to the second level of self-talk, instead of simply having the thought "I am fat," you might have evolved into thinking, "I need to lose weight." Or you might have a thought such as: "I should start exercising." Another common phrase used at this stage is, "I need to do …." Something to pay attention to here is that you can actually use this level of self-talk as a strategy for healing. If you are not experiencing this type of self-talk yet, and your self-talk remains mostly negative, try elevating things by moving to this type of self-talk on purpose, as a conscious exercise.

You can take this approach with all the levels of self-talk, in order to speed up the healing process. This works for many people, because it helps them to develop their abilities for positive thinking gradually and in stages, rather than trying to make a direct switch from negative to positive thinking. The types of statements at this level also help the conscious mind, because you are making a move from simply accepting the bad things in your life to recognizing that there is a need to make changes, and that more importantly, you are the agent of change.

For example, consider the following statement:

I can't lose weight. I am always going to be fat.

There are many ways that this statement can be turned into a statement that recognizes the need to make changes to improve the situation. Here is one way to do it:

I need to lose weight. I should start a diet that I am comfortable with.

This is a definite shift in thinking. Some people might proceed automatically through the levels of thought, but for most of us, making a conscious effort is going to be required.

In a definite sense, these types of thoughts are progress. Rather than simply being negative statements about our self-image, they have been changed into action statements. But, you will notice the phrases "I need ..." or "I should ...", and these are statements about the future without specific plans for taking action. And so, while we are making progress, this is far from an ideal situation.

One of the important steps to healing is not only recognizing that you are engaging in negative self-talk, but that you also take action to change it. So, when you are in a situation where you are saying to yourself: "I should do ..." or "I need to do ...", you are far from being healed when it comes to this problem. First of all, think of the phrase "I should ...." What are some of the things that this phrase conveys? I would say that one of the first things that comes to mind when I hear that phrase is that the person is not very serious about instituting change in their life. They have recognized that they have a problem, but they really haven't set a specific goal with a plan to reach that goal, in order to overcome the problem.

If you are in the stage where your thought processes are filled with a lot of "I should …" or "I need to …" type statements you need to write down each of these statements in a notebook. Then, for each statement of this type, develop a plan of action to start rectifying the problem. You want to break down your solution to each problem into three to five steps. So, this should be some type of practical approach that can actually be realized.

There are some types of negative self-talk that can be remedied by simply replacing them with positive thoughts. For example, "I'm ugly" is simply a statement. There isn't a practical approach that accompanies that statement. It's a relative statement that may or may not be based on reality at all. So, it's certainly one that is directly related to low self-esteem, and that should be replaced with a positive thought.

But if you find yourself engaging in any type of thought that could be characterized by the phrase "I should …" this is a thought that can be accompanied by action. That doesn't mean that we should automatically take action, however. You need to look at the thought process objectively and determine whether or not it really has validity. Sometimes, these types of thought processes are not valid. So, in those cases, you can simply throw them out by replacing them with positive thinking.

However, in some cases, those types of statements are going to be valid. Maybe you are ten pounds overweight. So, if you start saying to yourself "I should lose weight" rather than simply thinking "I am fat," it may be time to start taking action by writing down in your journal a plan to rectify the problem. Whatever plan you develop in your journal needs to have two steps. The first step is determining whether or not this is a real problem that is amenable to practical solutions. If not, you simply write down the positive statements to replace the negative thought. Then next time that you have negative thoughts, you replace them with a positive statement.

On the other hand, if this is something that you can act on, then write down the steps that you would take in order to rectify the problem. You should keep your steps in perspective. This means that you should set realistic goals that you can actually reach within a reasonable amount of time. Just to use one example to get a practical feel for this: suppose that you needed to lose 50 pounds. Losing 50 pounds is quite an achievement. So, as a matter of practicality, you probably aren't going to want to set losing 50 pounds as your goal. Instead, what you would do is set a goal of losing ten pounds and then come back to reevaluate the situation. For most goals, you can set down a three to five point plan and carry it out. I recommend putting specific dates in your plan, which will help to hold you accountable for actually carrying it out, and it will also help you get some perspective on the realistic possibilities that exist for solving the problem at hand.

Making a Decision to Change

The next level of self-talk is moving beyond phrases like "I should …" and actually making a decision to change. This is a major elevation in character. When you are ready to move up to this level of self-talk, you are well on your way to healing and reprogramming your mind to get rid of the negative "software" that has been operating for so long and directing your results without you even realizing it.

One characteristic of this level is that you are fully rejecting the victim status that comes with learned helplessness. Rather than seeing yourself as floating through the world and being impacted solely by outside forces like "luck," you recognize that you are an agent for control and change in your life. At each level of self-talk, we are reprogramming the subconscious mind in stages. In fact, at the previous level, we've already recognized that we are not a victim, but this level takes things further by marrying that realization to the belief that we have the power to control our own lives. At each level, as you practice the new statements to replace the old ones, be sure to use a lot of repetition. As we discussed earlier, the subconscious mind learns through repetition and the more that you use this technique, the stronger that something is going to hold.

With that in mind, I don't recommend moving to higher levels of self-talk until you are seeing definite signs that you are making progress at the previous level. The signs you want to look for include a change in attitude. This should include, more importantly, a change in the self-talk that you are actually experiencing. Don't move forward until you truly feel that you are ready.

Think about tennis players. If a budding tennis player can barely hit the ball, should they keep practicing hitting the ball with a forehand swing, or should they start learning backhands and killer serves? I think that the answer to this question is they should become competent with the most basic forehand swing before moving on to learn more advanced methods. And what is happening in that case? We want the new tennis player to practice until the forehand swing enters the realm of the subconscious.

The same procedure is going to be used here. But when you are ready, you can start moving forward and improving your self-talk at this level. Let's go back and review what we did in the last level.

Writing a plan in your self-talk journal should indicate a duty to do something, but it does not indicate an actual decision to move forward and carry out the action. So, the next step in self-talk is to replace phrases by "I will ...", "I will not ..." and "never." These are phrases that indicate a definite course of action.

Try going through this by looking at the negative self-talk that you have written in your journal. Are there any negative thoughts that could be replaced by "I should ..." and then "I will ..." types of statements?

Here is an example. Suppose that a person finds it difficult to get to work or meet friends on time. The negative self-talk that may accompany this could be something to the effect of:

I'm always late.

Notice that this is a general and definite statement, as it includes the word "always." You should look for definite statements like this that can be replaced, to turn a general statement about you into a specific statement about a specific situation. Returning to the present exercise, the first step to move up to the second level of self-talk would be something like this:

I should get to work five minutes early.

This change has done two things. It first acknowledges the "duty" or obligation for the behavior by including the phrase "I should ..." in the self-talk. The second thing that this change has done is it has turned a general comment about the person into a specific criticism that is constructive, rather than acting as an attack on self-esteem or worth.

You can actually work on your negative self-talk in real-time by using this technique, once you've identified the thought that you want to change. This is going to require some conscious awareness in regard to the negative self-talk that appears in your head. The adjusted phrase will essentially be used as an affirmation. When you get the negative thought, consciously replace it with the new thought. You can also use the statement in regular affirmation sessions.

After you have done this for a few days, you need to turn this into a level 3 statement, which is going to be a direct statement of action, or of making a change. In this example, our new phrase is going to be the following:

I will arrive at work five minutes early each day.

Now we have a definite statement that is geared toward actually changing the problem behavior. You can use this as an affirmation and also say it when you recognize the negative self-talk appearing in your head.

This example was directed at a simple problem that can be changed with a direct statement. But readers may be wondering how to apply this to more general issues related to self-esteem, financial problems, relationship problems, or appearance. The fact is, this method can be applied in any situation. Typically, negative self-talk will result when a specific event happens. So, you might say to yourself, *"I'm a loser,"* but the statement probably doesn't occur in isolation. Look at the situation that triggered the thought. Then put the self-talk in context so that it can be reframed.

Let's use a simple example. Suppose a teenage boy approaches the girl of his dreams and she rejects him. A natural reaction to have inside his head is: "I'm such a loser." This could be turned around using the above method, by injecting some different contexts into the statement. Because one girl rejected the boy, that doesn't mean he is a "loser" in any general sense. The boy could move to the "I should …" phase by saying, "I should find another girl to ask out. She probably already had a boyfriend." This change creates an obligation that helps to reframe the situation and get rid of the general comment on self-worth. In fact, by replacing the reaction "I'm such a loser" with "I should find another girl to ask out, she probably already had a boyfriend," we have turned the focus outward and added an action that would remedy the immediate situation that led to the negative self-talk in the first place. This way, the self-talk is not going to work against self-esteem, and it's not general.

You can use this technique in almost any situation. Suppose that you need to lose some weight, and you've recently gone on a strict diet. But you're at a restaurant with some friends, and when the waiter comes around tempting you with desserts, you decide to get a piece of the pie. Afterward, you are going to be flooded with negative feelings for having made this mistake. As a result, you might be saying things to yourself like "I'm such a loser" or "I never do anything right." You might experience negative self-talk that makes reference to your weight or body image. These types of thoughts will be accompanied by definite statements. For example, this type of negative self-talk might include "I'll never lose weight" or "I'm always going to be fat." So, while these statements are not general attacks on self-esteem, at least on the surface, they include definite statements that indicate accomplishing the goal is impossible for you. In a sense, even though they don't seem general on the surface, they really are general comments on your abilities and will act to lower self-esteem.

Once again, we can put this type of negative self-talk into context and reframe the message. The goal is to focus on specific behaviors rather than making general comments on our self-worth. The first step in a situation like this is to acknowledge the mistake made. This is a little different from the last hypothetical situation we examined; in that case, there was not a mistake. But here there is a definite action we can point to. So, in this situation, you can acknowledge the mistake and then pledge to yourself to make changes in the future. You could replace any of the negative-self talk statements above with something like:

I made a mistake in ordering dessert. Next time I should politely decline.

The statement can be changed into a definite plan of action by turning the phrase "I should" into "I will."

Can-Do Self-Talk (Better You)

The previous level of self-talk turned negative self-talk into a definite statement related to changing behavior. Now we want to turn it into the type of self-talk that gives you power to change and take control over your life. This level of self-talk can include definite statements about your capability to take action and positive statements about your self-worth. For example, "I am ..." is an important phrase in this level of self-talk, but rather than using it in a negative sense, you will use it in a positive statement.

I am smart and capable.

I am able to follow my diet and lose weight.

I am smart, interesting, and funny. I will get a date with the next girl.

I am in control of my financial life, and I am paying off my debts.

Any positive qualifier can be used at the can-do self-talk level. A common suggestion is to use the phrase: "Yes I can." This phrase includes a word that indicates definiteness, "Yes." It also includes a phrase with an assertion of your capacity to act: "I can."

Yes, I can stick to this diet and lose weight.

Yes, I can get to work five minutes early every day.

Universal Affirmation

The next level of self-talk elevates it to a spiritual level. This is the highest level of self-talk, and you should definitely move through all the previous levels before using universal self-talk. This level of self-talk can be used to express forgiveness, acceptance, and tolerance. This should begin with inward-directed thoughts. That is, you need to express forgiveness, acceptance, and tolerance toward yourself. Keep in mind that this is not an excuse for bad behaviors. Instead, it is a recognition that you are only human, and therefore you're going to be making mistakes. Forgiving yourself for making mistakes is a way to undo all the negative programming that has brought you to the point where you are now. Acceptance is a way to accept yourself for who you are. This is the opposite of saying, "I am such a loser." When you feel true acceptance, you realize that mistakes are going to be made in life but that these are not characteristic of you as a whole person, and they are not a reflection on your self-worth as a human being. Tolerance goes along with forgiveness. Again, this does not mean that you are endorsing the behaviors. This level of self-talk can be used in the form of affirmations that you say to yourself each day. Let's run through a couple of examples.

I am only human, and I forgive myself for making mistakes. I will do better next time.

I accept myself for who I am.

I accept myself and recognize I have flaws, but all human beings do.

You can also direct the universal affirmations outward.

Summary: The Five Levels of Self-Talk

Self-talk is an internal dialogue that tells us who we think we are. At this point, your internal self-talk is directed by years and even decades of negative programming that has been working in your subconscious mind, usually placed there or reinforced by external agents. These include your parents, caregivers, teachers, siblings, and peers. The five levels of self-talk explain different types of self-talk and give you a path forward that can be used to replace negative self-talk in a series of stages. This will turn the negative thinking into positive statements, and at first, it will take hard work and conscious effort. But like the tennis player who spends hours practicing, which turns their actions into automatic responses, the more you practice with the five levels of self-talk, the stronger and more automatic your positive self-talk is going to become. Remember that the subconscious mind is a blank slate, and I like to call it "dumb." That doesn't mean that the subconscious mind is not capable of producing large effects; if it couldn't, we wouldn't even be having this conversation. As we said earlier, by "dumb," I mean that the subconscious mind acts like a computer. It is ready to accept any programming that is given to it, and it will change accordingly. Of course, replacing old programming that has been ingrained for years is not easy, so have faith even if you don't get the results you want right away. Keep working at it until the old, negative programs are replaced by new can-do positive thinking.

Chapter 4: Stop the Blame Game

An unfortunate plague that can infect people with negative self-talk is the blame game. This can manifest in two different ways. The first way is in a constant effort by the person experiencing negative self-talk to blame other people and external factors for the circumstances they are in. So, you might blame your parents, or it's the fault of your boss that you have a lousy job. That would be in place of the rational view of the situation, which would be that if you have a job you don't like, find a new one instead of continuing to be in misery and focusing your energy on a lousy boss. We might recognize that having problems with your parents can influence your life, but it's something that you can overcome. This type of blame allows you to avoid taking responsibility for your situation.

Those whose lives are dominated by negative self-talk also blame themselves. In fact, some people fall squarely in this camp. Having low self-esteem is often accompanied by blaming yourself for everything that happens. One theme I have been emphasizing in this book is that you are an active agent capable of controlling your own future, but that doesn't mean that you have to blame yourself for each and every single situation. Self-blame is also not done in a constructive fashion. Instead, it is done in a way that reinforces negative thinking and serves to lower self-esteem even further. It will take the form of statements like: "I can't do anything right."

Blaming Someone Else for Your Problems

One of the reasons that people blame others for their circumstances is that they don't want to point the finger at themselves and lower their self-esteem even further. Remember that this all happens at the level of the subconscious, and the people who are experiencing this are not even aware that it's happening. It is human nature to want to protect your self-esteem and the image of yourself in your mind, even if you are plagued by negative thinking and already have low self-esteem. This can be called the fragile ego effect. It's also a result of dysfunctional thinking, in that the person with healthy thought processes would recognize that if they accept blame for a situation, that doesn't make them a bad person. Bad results from one incident or situation do not mean that you are a bad person overall or that you have no self-worth.

However, if you have dysfunctional thought processes related to self-esteem, you are prone to associate one mistake or bad action with the total destruction of your self-worth. So, in order to protect yourself from that kind of injury, you will project your blame outward.

Blaming someone else for our problems is a fairly common dysfunction. You can randomly approach people on the street, and it won't take long before you find someone who can blame others for their circumstances. We already gave a common example. How hard is it to find a person who will blame their boss for a poor work environment? If you dig deeper, you are likely to find that this person blames others for different circumstances in their life.

For this kind of person, everything bad that happens is somebody else's fault. It also protects them from the need to make changes to the way they think and live. So, the guy who says his lousy work-life is the fault of his boss also blames the banks or credit card companies for his massive debt that makes it hard for him to pay the bills each month. It's always going to be someone else that is the root cause of all his problems. If he is married, then it's going to be his wife's fault. The blame game is a convenient defense mechanism because you can always find an external agent on which to cast blame. The blame game can be said to be a mentality where "anyone but me" is at fault. This is an interesting expression of negative self-talk, that while rooted in low self-esteem, it expresses itself through projection, casting blame on others who might have some influence in your life, whether they are at fault or not. Usually, in interpersonal relations, unless it's a situation that involves outright abuse, both people are contributing. Why not look at your own contributions to bad situations instead of casting the blame on others?

Are you partaking in the blame game?

Start looking at the bad situations in your life. Write them down on a sheet of paper. Maybe you have too much debt that you aren't able to pay off. Maybe you hate your job. Write all of these situations down—but don't write down the rational explanation for them. Write down the thoughts you've been telling yourself about them. Note when you are blaming someone else.

The first step in a "blaming others" situation is to take a step back and try to look at the situation objectively. This is not an easy thing to do. But the key here is to look at the role you are playing in the situation.

If you hate your job and blame your boss, who is difficult to get along with, there are several questions you can ask yourself. Is the problem really your boss? What role are you playing in your relationship with the boss? Maybe you show up to work late, or maybe you work at a slow and unproductive pace. Maybe when the boss criticizes you, you tend to take it personally (very common among those who are suffering from negative self-talk). Try and think of the roles that you are actually playing in the situation and in your relationships that could be contributing to the problem.

If you are able to identify some ways that you are contributing to the problem, then take it to the next step. Write down the opposite behaviors that would end your contribution to the problem. It might be as simple as changing the tone of voice you use when your boss criticizes you for something. Instead of reacting negatively, thank her for pointing out the things you were doing wrong, and promise to work harder to improve your performance. If you are showing up to work late, start showing up to work early. Try to find at least three situations that are within your power to change.

The next step is to implement the new behaviors for a month. Think about it; a month is not really a long time at all. See how it goes for a month, and then re-evaluate your relationship with your boss and your feelings about the job after making the changes. Even if you don't see an improvement, this is a good exercise in avoiding casting blame, and instead focusing on taking action to implement changes. However, chances are you are going to see improvement in the dynamics of the interaction along with a better overall feeling about the job and the relationship you are having with your boss.

If your job is objectively lousy, ask yourself what you are doing about it. Are you even looking for a new job? Or are you simply running in place, and then continually complaining about it?

When it comes to interpersonal interactions, blaming those who are closest to us for our problems is quite a common occurrence. How many people have blamed their parents for where they are in their lives now? Let's be clear—your parents can have a very big influence, and if it was not positive, then the negative programming that they plugged into your subconscious mind can be causing problems. But are they at fault, decades later? If you are an adult, it's time for you to take responsibility for the position that you are in with your life at this very moment. That doesn't mean completely forgetting the negative programming that was put into your subconscious by others when you were a child, but you need to take responsibility for reprogramming your subconscious and avoid casting blame on others. You are not a victim.

Another common method of deflection that is used is called labeling. In fact, we've been seeing self-directed labeling throughout the book. Labeling takes the form of attaching some general, self-defeating characteristic to yourself. A common example is to say: "I am stupid." But labeling can also play a role in the blame game when you deflect blame onto others. In a work situation or interpersonal relationship, when casting blame on the people around us, we also label them, for example: "My wife is stubborn." If you see that you are using labeling to put other people in boxes, you should adjust your thinking, in the same way that you would adjust your thinking for your own negative self-talk. In fact, this is just another example of self-talk, even though it's directed toward others, and its purpose is to absolve yourself from taking responsibility.

Try looking for actions you are taking that could lead to the apparent validity of the attribute that you have given as a label to someone. So maybe we can turn "My wife is stubborn" into:

My wife won't talk when I yell.

This statement recognizes that there is behavior exhibited by the wife that could be interpreted as her being stubborn, but it has also recognized the role that you are playing in the situation. We can use this in other situations as well.

My boss is a jerk.

After determining actions that you are taking to cause your boss to behave in an abrasive manner, you might say this instead:

My boss is short-tempered when I show up to work late.

This identifies your own behavior that may have contributed to the situation. Of course, this does not completely absolve your boss. If you start showing up to work early and your boss continues to be short-tempered, then maybe your boss does have issues. But in that case, it is still your responsibility to fix the situation—in this case, by finding a new job that is a better fit for you.

Sometimes casting blame takes the form of abstractions. So, there isn't really a specific person to blame. Maybe you are not making enough money to make ends meet. Instead of taking action by looking for a second job or working more hours, or working toward getting a promotion and higher pay, you blame the external circumstances. You'll blame the job itself, or blame the company, rather than looking for ways to improve your own situation.

Casting blame on others for your circumstances is no minor issue. It's a major flaw in your thought processes, and it's going to be holding you back in your life. If you are finding that you are often blaming others for your circumstances or bad things that happen in your life, it's time to change this way of thinking. Start by writing down any occasion when you catch yourself blaming others or attributing blame in an abstract sense. Then write down the role that you are playing in each situation. Once you have figured that out, write down the steps you can take to change your role in the situation. This is not a guarantee that the situation will change, but certainly, in most cases, it will improve. But remember you can't just write down the steps for change—you are going to need to actually carry them out.

Blaming Yourself

The other extreme is blaming yourself for everything. The last section does illuminate the fact that when there are conflicts and bad situations, we often play a role in the circumstances. However, it's also true that we are not to blame for every single thing that happens. Self-blame can be as destructive as blaming others. There is a fine line between taking responsibility for making mistakes and blaming yourself for everything that happens. If you are facing negative self-talk and the destructive thought processes and attitudes that go along with it, this can mean that blaming yourself for everything is part of the dysfunctional pattern and will only lead to lower self-esteem.

Blaming yourself takes a familiar form. Self-blame will include statements like "I should have done …" or "If only I had done …

then ...." You will constantly be telling yourself: "It's my fault this happened."

Again, there is a fine line, because it's important to recognize that in many cases, bad things that happen are our own fault. But besides recognizing that we contribute to situations and that many people or circumstances might be responsible, the way that we react to situations that we are at fault for is as important as the recognition itself.

The unhealthy way to respond to this kind of situation is to see that you are at fault, blame yourself, and then wallow in depression about it. This is usually accompanied by a general crash in self-esteem. The healthy way to respond to a situation that you played a role in creating is to acknowledge the mistakes you made, and then make a plan to learn from the mistakes and do better next time. You should acknowledge the mistakes you make without blaming yourself and without blowing the mistakes out of proportion, so that they don't turn into an overall evaluation of your worth as a human being.

If you feel that you are at fault for a bad outcome or event that has happened, and other people are involved, try offering an apology for your actions. Don't make a big deal about it but apologize. If possible, include an action that will help to rectify the situation with your apology. This will help mend your relationships with other people and can prompt expressions of forgiveness. It will also promote tolerance and acceptance among those who are around you. They are going to appreciate the fact that when you have made a mistake, you are willing to take responsibility for it. The positive energy that this will create will help to elevate your good and positive feelings, and that, in turn, will help to direct your self-talk in a more positive direction.

When you are suffering from the first level of negative self-talk, your subconscious is directing your mood and actions through negative programming. One side effect of this is that negative events are not time-limited in your mind. This is a result of the fact that you tend to blow things out of proportion. It's also a result of generalizing. So, if you made a mistake at work that caused a lot of problems, you'll generalize it to impact your overall feelings of self-esteem and self-worth. These feelings are, in a sense, permanent and timeless without intervention. Therefore, you will remove the time-limited aspect that should be associated with the problem, and you might even make it permanent. Relatively minor bad events are normally localized in nature, and healthy people move on from them in a short time. But if your mindset is dominated by negative programming, you might find this difficult or impossible.

Affirmations can help here. Use affirmations that acknowledge that you made a mistake, but that you will do better next time and you're moving on. Also, redirect your mind. As each day passes, new situations and issues arise. If you find your mind wandering back to the troublesome event, remind yourself that it was in the past and doesn't matter anymore, and replace the thoughts about it by current concerns, no matter how minor they are.

Manipulative Blame

Another unhealthy way to use the blame game is to do so in a manipulative fashion. If you are engaging in this type of behavior, it is probably happening on an unconscious level, so you should forgive yourself for doing so. But it is important to recognize this behavior and end it, because blaming either yourself or others in a manipulative way is a toxic behavior.

In rare cases, people who are narcissistic or sociopathic will use blame in a conscious manner in order to manipulate people. However, we are going to ignore that for the purposes of this discussion. If you find someone in your life that is engaging in that kind of behavior, that is someone that you definitely want to avoid.

One way that manipulative blame is used is to generate sympathy. So, in this case, it's going to be self-blame. Again, we are ignoring the case of a sociopath that consciously uses this as a "technique" to manipulate others, that kind of topic is beyond the scope of this book. What we are talking about here are otherwise normal people who are suffering from low self-esteem and negative thought processes. In this case, you aren't really conscious of doing it, but you will blame yourself in order to draw the sympathy of others, in a misguided attempt to get others to pay attention to you and reinforce your self-esteem.

This is a hard one to accept and move past, but if you find yourself engaging in this type of behavior, forgive yourself. Adopt an attitude of tolerance and acceptance and pledge to avoid doing it in the future. Becoming aware of the behavior is the first step that you can take in your journey to interacting with others in a healthier fashion. When you are in a situation where you are feeling the urge to accept blame, and you can recognize when it might be a case of actually directing sympathy toward yourself, consciously recognize the self-talk that is going on at the time leading you toward taking this kind of action. Use that to replace it with thoughts that are more positive and uplifting.

Another case of manipulative blame is immediately casting blame on others, to avoid taking the responsibility yourself. Of course, we have discussed this situation in the context of self-talk, but in this situation, we are considering the person who does this publicly so that blame is actually shifted. Again, the first step is recognition of the problem. If you are doing this, become consciously aware of the situation and the negative thought processes that can cause you to take negative actions that impact others. Replace these thoughts by more positive thoughts, and also thoughts that increase your own self-responsibility.

Chapter 5: Confronting Negative Self Talk

In this chapter, we are going to focus more closely on the process of confronting negative self-talk for the purpose of eliminating it. This is an important step in the process of healing yourself from years of negative programming. The first step in confronting negative self-talk is to recognize it when it happens in real-time. This can actually be a very difficult process. Think about all the years that have gone by and you've been experiencing negative self-talk, and all of this is going on at a subconscious level. That means the most basic step of all, which is simply recognizing negative self-talk when it occurs, can be very difficult for some people. But if you are willing to put the required work in to do this, you will make progress on this issue very quickly.

Once you have recognized negative self-talk, you need to know what to do with it. The purpose here is to label it and replace it with positive self-talk.

Recognizing Negative Self-Talk

It's one thing to talk about negative self-talk in a book, or even to write down some negative self-talk that you've experienced, in a journal. It can be quite another thing to actually recognize it in real-time. Since this is so difficult, it's going to take some work. The fact is you have gone your entire life experiencing negative thoughts flowing through your mind without actually being aware that it's happening. So, it's hard to focus when these thoughts are just unconsciously flowing through your mind—often when you're busy with other things. The easiest way to recognize negative self-talk is when it happens in a specific situation. For example, somebody may upset you, or maybe you made a mistake of some kind.

That is hard enough as it is to do in real-time. It's even worse when you're not directly involved in a bad situation, but you're having negative thoughts that are often quite subtle in nature, flowing through your head throughout the day. You might be having negative thoughts while driving to work, or when you're sitting at your desk going through emails. Or you might have negative thoughts if you're doing something as simple as browsing Facebook. So, in these situations, your mind is focused on the task at hand, and the negative thoughts are occurring in the background. In that case, it may be hard to recognize them. Of course, when you are in the midst of a bad experience, it will be easier to recognize the negative thoughts that are occurring in relation to that experience.

The first step that you can take is to have awareness. Part of that awareness is to familiarize yourself with the kinds of words and phrases that commonly appear in negative self-talk. It's impossible to present an exhaustive list, but you can write down your own list and see what you come up with. Some of the words that could be included are: stupid, dumb, inept, failure, wrong, if only, I wish, I always, I can't, perfect, what's the point, there is no use, I'm not worthy, I'm a loser, I'm not worth it, I'll never change, I can't change, and things will never change.

Try sitting down and seeing if you can expand this list, using your own negative thoughts as a guide.

Catching Yourself Using Negative Self-Talk

The first step that you need to use in this process is catching yourself in the act. You're going to have to put in some effort, and I am talking about conscious effort, to catch yourself engaging in the negative self-talk. So, each morning when you get up you should meditate on this for a few minutes. Commit yourself to recognizing negative self-talk when it occurs throughout the day. As I said in the last section, this is not going to be easy, so you can forgive yourself ahead of time for missing a lot of the negative self-talk that happens on autopilot.

However, after you start committing to doing this, you are going to find that it will become easier to spot negative thoughts as they occur. This is going to require a heightened sense of self-awareness. I have to say that there are going to be multiple benefits that you will experience in engaging in this exercise.

Begin by simply recognizing when the negative thought occurs. Then, make a conscious effort to make a statement reflecting the negative thoughts back. So, let's just say that a negative thought is: "I am a loser." When you notice yourself saying this, pause for a minute and then say to yourself (in your mind if necessary), "I just had the thought that I am a loser."

Although we are anxious to see improvement in our lives, when we take things a little bit slowly, we do a more thorough job in healing, and we will see better results down the road. Therefore, you should practice simply recognizing the negative thoughts and self-talk that you're having throughout the day, and pause to notice them on a conscious level. Do this for about a week. You will find that as time goes on and you practice this skill more, you will catch more and more negative thoughts as they flow through your head. This will help you to defeat them and replace them with positive thoughts later on.

Negative thought patterns and self-talk can often cause a higher level of stress on the body. If you notice that you are feeling tense, achy, or tired when having a lot of negative thoughts, then as you recognize them do some deep breathing exercises. Begin to increase your awareness that the supposed "truths" contained in the negative self-talk are not truths at all, but are usually in fact exaggerations if not outright false statements. This kind of recognition will help to bring down the stress level that negative self-talk creates. It will lessen the impact of the negative self-talk, both mentally and physically.

Labeling Negative Self-Talk

You should use multiple types of labeling when addressing negative thoughts. In addition to labeling your negative self-talk as "just a thought," you can label the statement as "false." For example, consider the following negative statement:

I can't speak up during the meeting, because I will sound stupid.

Let's label this statement as nothing more than a thought, and then make sure that we emphasize that it's not true. So, we could say:

I just had the thought that if I speak up in the meeting, I will sound stupid. It's not true.

Now we have taken the process of recognizing our negative self-talk two steps further. By labeling the self-talk as a "thought," we work to diminish its importance. Second, we have recognized that it is not a true statement.

Telling Your Negative Thoughts to F-Off

We can carry this exercise a step further. After you have labeled the negative thought, you can tell it to go away. How you go about doing this is up to you, but basically, you want to tell the thought to disappear from your mind. You can do this with a simple wave of the hand in the beginning.

Spend a few days attacking your negative thoughts in this manner. Simply getting rid of them and minimizing their importance is a major step forward. The more time that your mind spends without negative thoughts, the better off you will be. In fact, this is a positive in and of itself, even though you might not have replaced it with a positive thought.

As part of the process of getting rid of negative self-talk, you can carefully examine the statements that are causing you the most trouble. Remember that people who are suffering from negative self-talk and the types of programming that give rise to it, are often the kinds of people who make mountains out of molehills. In other words, they blow things out of proportion and overreact. Take a look at the situations that give rise to your own negative self-talk and see if you aren't engaging in this type of behavior yourself. Also, I recall our discussion about the time-limiting nature of most mistakes and problems. Each time that you find yourself having a negative thought, ask yourself if this is a problem that is going to be causing problems over the long-term.

Second, don't make assumptions. One problematic response that people engage in, which leads to negative thoughts, is making assumptions about the intentions of others. When your subconscious mind is governed by negative programming, this usually takes the form of assuming that other people are thinking negative thoughts about you. In fact, these can be specific instances of negative self-talk. "I know she thinks I am stupid," or "My manager thinks I am worthless." Try catching yourself in these kinds of negative thought patterns as well. While you are not directly labeling yourself, in reality, you are still engaging in labeling, but you are projecting the labeling onto others. So instead of calling yourself stupid, you are asserting to yourself that someone else thinks you are stupid when you would usually have no objective evidence that this is really the case.

Of course, this reminds us that we should eliminate generalized labels from our self-talk. So, you want to eliminate things like "I am completely hopeless" or "I am stupid" from your self-talk.

Also, avoid the all-or-nothing fallacy that comes along with black-and-white thinking. There are very few situations that fall into this category, so you want to get that type of thinking out of your mind in most circumstances. Don't view a single event in your life as either all good or all bad, and don't inflate the importance of any one event. Most events are very time-limited and don't have that big of an impact. Have some awareness of when this is the case.

Changing Perspectives

This is difficult to do, but when you are troubled by a situation or event, try putting yourself in someone else's shoes. It might not be easy to see yourself from other perspectives, so instead, you might want to try imagining how your behavior would look if someone else did it. Maybe you were at work, and you made a remark in a meeting that everyone seemed to ignore. So, you tell yourself how stupid you are, and that you should just avoid speaking up in meetings so that you won't reinforce the perception that you are dumb. Catch yourself in these thoughts and label them and tell them to go away. Then imagine one of your coworkers speaking up as you did. When you do this, it will help you to realize how minor the event really was, and you will recognize that you would not have thought that the person was "stupid" for having spoken up. This will make it a little bit easier to see that you also aren't looking that way to others. Try using a change of perspective whenever the interaction involves multiple people. This is also going to help you see the time-limited nature that characterizes many interactions that we blow out of proportion in our own minds.

Changing perspective can also help you communicate more effectively and in a healthier manner in general, by the way. For those times that you did actually make a mistake in your communication, it helps if you can try seeing it from someone else's perspective.

Replacing Negative Thoughts

The final step in this process is to start training your mind to have positive thoughts instead. This process can be a bit nuanced. Remember that in the last chapter we discussed how easy it is to blame other people for our own situations, and so sometimes we have to replace our negative thoughts while recognizing the role that we play in creating our own reality. In this case, it is not going to be some feel-good session of just talking yourself up. You should work to replace the negative thoughts you are having with positive thoughts that are realistic in what they say.

To get started, we need to consider how a healthy person engages in positive thinking. Simply wishing upon a star is not something that can be called "healthy." So, you should not engage in artificial self-esteem building, and you don't want to set up pie in the sky expectations that are impossible to realize. You should also avoid vague generalizations.

Keep in mind that generalized positive thoughts like "I'm good enough" or "I am smart and confident" are good to include in your affirmations. In this case, we are talking about replacing specific negative thoughts that are occurring in your daily life, often about specific issues and situations.

Positive self-talk should affirm your value without being egocentric. It should be supportive while recognizing the mistakes you make and the role that you play in different situations. Positive self-talk will often invoke a specific plan that can actually be accomplished. It will recognize the mistakes that occur and rather than using them to punish yourself and emphasize your own lack of self-worth, positive self-talk will focus on generating a plan of action to correct the mistakes and move forward.

Let's look at some negative and positive self-talk examples for a few situations, to see ways that you can turn around negative self-talk and replace it with a positive statement. A positive statement, as we said above, isn't necessarily going to be a completely win-win statement or something that puts your head in the clouds, it will be a realistic statement that can recognize problems without completely destroying your own self-esteem and self-worth.

Here is an example of a negative statement:

I am so stupid! I should just keep my mouth shut in meetings. Nobody even heard what I said. I looked like a total weirdo.

This could be replaced by a more realistic statement, such as:

I know I can do better. I am going to practice speaking louder and more clearly so that people will be able to hear what I have to say. I have interesting and insightful things to share in our meetings.

Another example of a negative thought:

I am not going to bother dieting anymore! I cheat every time. I am never going to lose weight!

This can be replaced by a more realistic positive statement:

I made a mistake in eating dessert. Next time I am going to refuse it, and I am going to devote more time to exercise.

The difference between a negative self-talk statement and a positive self-talk statement isn't so much that we are simply feeling good about ourselves, but instead, we are removing personal attacks that we make on ourselves and our own self-worth. These are replaced by facts about the situation, possibly including the recognition that we made a mistake, and then a plan of action to do better in the future.

Negative self-talk avoids any suggestion that there is a way to solve the problems at hand. It simply focuses on destroying whatever self-esteem you have left, and turns a generalization from a single error into a feeling of complete unworthiness. When you engage in negative self-talk, the interpretation of the situation is completely unrealistic, blown out of proportion, and made completely general.

Consider a professional basketball player—let us suppose that they are married and have children at home. One day the player has a bad game, and continually makes mistakes in the game. Positive self-talk after the game would recognize the problems that were specific to that one situation. So, the player might say, "I should practice more, and make sure I get a good night's sleep before the game." This type of self-talk is realistic and offers a prescription that is specific to that situation—performing badly in one single game. If the player had negative self-talk, they might say to themselves "I'm such a loser! I should just quit the team! My children probably don't want even to see me, so maybe I won't even go home!"

That kind of generalization is completely unrealistic. Although this might be seen as an extreme example, when you look at your own self-talk, you'll see that the highlighted reaction is also not really an exaggeration. You might be engaging in that kind of self-talk on a daily basis yourself. It's easy to see how ridiculous it is when we imagine someone else engaging in negative self-talk—particularly when they are in a high position of achievement like "professional basketball player." But this helps to illustrate how imagining others having the same thoughts and feelings can help you put your self-talk in perspective.

Getting Rid of Negative Self-Talk and Replacing it Can Change How You Feel

The first few times you recognize your negative self-talk and then eliminate it, think about how this makes you feel. You are probably going to find that this relieves the amount of stress that you are feeling in your life and that it's also going to improve your self-esteem. In a small way, it is taking control of your own life. And actually, it's quite a big improvement, because taking control over your self-talk is a way to change the entire direction of your life.

You can then see how changing your self-talk by replacing negative thoughts with positive statements changes the way that you feel. Pay attention to not only how it makes you feel, but also see if you start noticing the direction of your life changing. At first, you might start to see that your behavior is changing as a result of the new programming that you are instilling in your mind. As a result of your new behaviors, you are probably also going to see better life results.

Chapter 6: Fostering Self Esteem

A large part of overcoming the negative programming that has been a part of your life for so many years, involves fostering your own self-esteem. You want to reach a point where your self-esteem is positive and healthy without being narcissistic. That means you need to recognize your own value and contributions while having a realistic interpretation of them. One of the problems has been the negative programming that you've been experiencing; it essentially makes you your own bully.

People who have negative programming and engage in negative self-talk are constantly putting themselves down. You don't need anyone else to do it for you—you are your own worst enemy. So, you need to start there by ending the self-criticism that constantly puts you down. From here, you can start fostering self-worth and self-esteem and then become, what I like to call, "a leader of self."

Stop Being Your Own Bully

The worst thing about negative programming in the self-talk that it generates is that we are constantly putting ourselves down. The criticism that we offer ourselves is general in nature, and so we reject our own self-value and our own uniqueness. This is a theme that has been running through the book, but it bears repeating. The problem with negative self-talk—among other things—is that the criticism that it engenders actually puts you down as a person, rather than focusing on specific mistakes or errors that you have made. I'm sure that you recognize in other people the fact that they can still have value even when they make a mistake. The problem is that you are not holding yourself to your own standards.

Recognizing Yourself as Worthy

The first step in healing, so that you can foster self-esteem, is recognizing that you have your own self-worth. You are a unique human being that is as special as anyone else. It's true that you have your own flaws, but we all do. You also have your own strengths and skills that have been combined in a completely unique way, which makes you a special individual.

Try developing some affirmations that focus on the strengths that you know you have. You can say these to yourself a couple of times a day to recognize your own worthiness as a human being. You can also try to keep them in mind to use, in order to replace negative thoughts that you have about your own self-worth during the day.

Steps to Foster Self-Love and Self-Esteem

Often times, negative thought processes and self-talk arise when you have had a negative experience of some type. Maybe you made a mistake, or you perceive that you made a mistake. Or maybe you've had a conflict with somebody. Many times, when we get in arguments, if we have low levels of self-love and self-esteem, we will be prone to blaming ourselves and feeling negative.

One important way to deal with these situations is to focus on the issue at hand, and the specific behaviors themselves, without focusing on yourself as a person. That way, you can reject the mistake or the behavior that you may have engaged in, while still recognizing your value as a person. This will help to keep your self-esteem intact, even when you've made bad decisions or behaved in a bad manner.

Something else that you need to do is not bring up things that happened in the past in the context of current situations. Often times, as we've noted, people who are suffering from negative programming have a tendency to dwell on the past. Once again, I'm not saying to forget the past, but don't use current difficulties as an excuse to bring up the past and punish yourself for doing it again.

Another problem that we all have—to one extent or another—is comparing ourselves to other people. This is a mental exercise that you should avoid engaging in. Comparing yourself to others unless you are looking to them for inspiration is not helpful. You don't want to be comparing yourself to other people if you are going to end up putting yourself down in the process. This only serves to tear down whatever self-esteem that you may have. So, something to avoid is looking at another person and saying: "Well, they always get it right, and I always get it wrong." That is not a helpful way to compare yourself to another person.

And in fact, if you are looking to other people for inspiration, you shouldn't do it in the manner of comparing yourself to them. Instead, you should use them as an example of how you could change the way you act in certain situations, or maybe you're inspired by the level of education or training somebody has obtained. In that case, you might say to yourself: "Well, I can do what they do when they are in a difficult situation," or alternatively "I'm going to get the kind of education that they got." You should reframe any examples that involve other people and where they are positioned in their life, rather than simply comparing yourself to them in order to put yourself down.

Another thing to consider in these types of situations is the fact that your negative outlook on life reflects itself as a negative thought process. You should start looking at the positives instead. Let's refer back to the chapter where I discussed a set of dysfunctional ways to look at situations that I called "the reality distortion field." If you recall, one of the dysfunctional ways of interpreting situations that psychologists have identified is called filtering. To refresh your memory, what happens is that people who engage in filtering tend to focus on the negative aspects of a situation. And so, what happens in these people is they ignore the positives that are sure to be there in any experience.

Are you doing this in your own life?

Try filtering the other direction. I don't want to emphasize this too much because I don't want to get into a "goody-feely" type of outlook. So, in other words, I'm not going to advise that you do filtering and only focus on the positive aspects of an interaction or situation. There may be negative things happening that you need to be aware of in order to learn from your mistakes. But what I am saying is that you should keep your eye out for the positives as well as the negatives and give yourself credit where credit is due. This is especially true when you are working on changing yourself and improving your situation. That's because when we are learning, we are still going to be more prone to seeing negative aspects of the situation and even toward making more mistakes than usual. One of the reasons that we make more mistakes is that if we are constantly blaming others or engaging with negative thoughts, there is no reason to improve ourselves. So, don't be discouraged if it's harder to find positive aspects of the situation. Be happy when you find them and praise yourself for them.

Let's take a couple of practical examples. Earlier in the book, we used the example of speaking out in a meeting, and maybe that's not something you normally do. So perhaps you were nervous and didn't speak loud enough for people to hear you clearly, and so they might not have said anything in response, and it appeared that they were ignoring you or not valuing what you had to say. When discussing this situation earlier, I mentioned that you could replace your interpretation of the event with a pledge to do better next time. But there are also positives in this experience. If you have previously been nervous about speaking up in meetings, even if the particular event did not go well, you should congratulate yourself for having the courage to speak out. You should also remind yourself that your opinions and your contributions matter.

Another important step in fostering your self-esteem is recognizing that things don't always progress in a linear fashion. So, you are not going to get rid of your negative self-talk all in one go. You are also not going to feel better about all your situations or change your bad behaviors in a perfectly consistent manner that progresses from day to day. It's going to be important to recognize that sometimes you're going to take a step forward, while other times you might find yourself taking two steps back. But at other times, you are going to take three steps forward and make serious progress.

And the truth is that even when you have setbacks, you are still making progress. Once you get going on this, remember that it wasn't that long ago when you were completely trapped by your negative thought processes. When things don't seem to be going the right way, don't worry about it and just keep on doing the exercises.

You can also always refer to your self-talk journal. Don't just keep a journal for the sake of recording negative thoughts. Also, record the positive thoughts and changes in behavior that you are seeing. That way, you can use the journal to help yourself get a more realistic view of how things are progressing. Imagine that at the start of a new week you have several days in a row of bad experiences and negative thoughts that you can't seem to get out of. In a situation like that, you might consider going back to the journal and reviewing your past progress. This will help boost your mood and self-esteem, and help you realize that progress is going to involve some occasional setbacks. This way, you can avoid getting all down and depressed about it.

Take Up Hobbies or Volunteer

One of the things that often contributes to negative thought processes is a mild level of depression. So many people who are suffering from negative self-talk are slightly depressed. But they are not really depressed enough to possibly even notice it or even get treatment for it. For that kind of low-level depression, going on medication is certainly not recommended in any situation. Instead, you should look to change your external life, to help foster good feelings and purpose in life.

One way that you can do this is by taking up some hobbies or volunteering. Many people will read this and start grumbling that they don't have time. Try not to make excuses—and find the time when you can do something. If you aren't sure about what you might be interested in, get out a piece of paper and write down different activities or sports, or passions that could be used for volunteering. Then figure out how to get involved in doing these, maybe just once or twice a week.

This will have a great impact on your life. For one thing, it will help you to make more connections with other people in situations that are not really judgmental. For example, if you take up a hobby that is innocuous, like bird watching, this is something that you can just do for fun and to meet other people without worrying about acquiring some massive skill set and impressing people. I also encourage people to take up activities that get them outdoors.

Two of the side benefits of this include elevating your mood. Simply engaging with other people in a shared activity that doesn't involve work or family responsibilities is going to go a long way toward elevating your mood. Second, if you can get one or more hobbies that involve being outdoors, this alone is going to help elevate your mood. You are also going to find your mind distracted a bit by your interest in the hobby.

The end result of this is that you are going to find yourself feeling better about yourself. Your mind is going to have less time to engage in negative thinking, and the elevation of your mood is actually going to change the state of your brain so that you will naturally drift toward higher levels of self-love and self-esteem.

Perhaps the ideal situation would be to take up one hobby and one volunteering interest. By volunteering, you can help take some of the focus off yourself and turn it toward a cause that is greater than self. It really doesn't matter what you pick, but it should have some kind of higher purpose. Volunteering will help you connect with like-minded folks, and the shared passion about the cause will help to alleviate negative thinking patterns. It's also going to help elevate your self-esteem, in part because you are getting some new purpose in your life, while also getting involved in something that has a larger purpose beyond just individual matters. One of the problems that we have in our society today is that there is an excessive focus on activities that are only designed to entertain us individually. So, we are spending too much time watching Netflix, listening to music, trying to develop the perfect body, or playing video games. In my view, it can go a long way if you spend a little bit of time focused outward instead of inward.

Building a Foundation of Self-Esteem

In order to build a foundation of self-esteem, you should start by adopting an attitude of unconditional love. This might sound a little bit strange, but you're going to need to apply that unconditional love to yourself. If you don't love yourself and accept yourself the way you are, nobody else is going to be able to love or respect you either.

Unconditional love means that you love yourself the way you are and accept the fact that you are not perfect. When you make mistakes, you need to recognize them within this type of context.

Tolerance and acceptance are part of unconditional love. You should also forgive yourself for wrongdoing. Again, this does not mean that you allow yourself to get by continually making wrong decisions or making mistakes without learning from them. What we are after here is not conflating bad behavior with the person. As part of this exercise, you might learn to do that with other people.

In some cases, people that are really hard on themselves are also hard and extra judgmental when it comes to their opinions about other people. So, you can also work on building a foundation for your own self-esteem by applying these principles to other people. You might even do it to the people that you have the most difficulties in your life with, such as your boss at work. Be forgiving and understand that sometimes people interact in unhealthy ways because of problems they are having at home. Your boss could have a serious illness that you don't know about, or maybe she just had an argument with her husband before coming to work. A coworker may be having financial problems that make them a little bit grouchy.

And of course, other people besides yourself simply make mistakes. So, try adopting an attitude of forgiveness, tolerance, and acceptance, and apply it to yourself and also to those around you.

Another way to foster self-esteem is to drop the expectations you have from others. That doesn't mean that you become a rug and let people walk all over you. You should definitely demand respect and decent treatment from other people. But stop expecting other people to acknowledge your achievements or contributions. Be happy when they do but ignore it when they don't. A lot of times, we set ourselves up for negative self-talk and thought processes if we expect too much out of other people. One of the most important things that I learned is that other people don't always have you as the focus in their life. They have a lot of other things on their mind, and so you might be number ten on their list. This is not a reflection on your inherent value or importance. So, don't take it that way, but just realize all the mistakes and errors that you make in your interactions with others are not necessarily as important to them as they are to you. This is going to help foster self-esteem because then you will realize that sometimes when other people aren't reacting to you, it has nothing to do with you at all, and there's no reason to engage in negative thought processes as a result.

Becoming a Leader of Self

Realizing that you have the power to control your own life is one of the most important steps to eliminating negative self-talk and thoughts from your mind. It's important to recognize that when you have the power to control your own life, while it's not complete power, you do have some control over the outcomes that you experience. This is a very different attitude than attributing everything to luck or connections. It's also very empowering. However, it comes with a certain level of taking responsibility.

If you have the power to control your own life and its outcomes, that means you need to take responsibility when things are not going the way that you want them to. This can be hard for some people to accept. Especially if you were going through your life blaming other people for the situation and circumstances that you are in now. In fact, the concept of blame has no place when you take responsibility for yourself.

Taking responsibility means that you are going to take the correct actions that are necessary in order to get good outcomes. Keep in mind that no outcome is guaranteed. However, you are still going to need to take the right steps to make progress in your life. When you're doing this, the outcomes will depend a lot more on you, as opposed to sitting around having negative thoughts that prevent you from taking action.

Taking responsibility also means righting the ship when you have made mistakes that hurt others. So be prepared to admit your mistakes to yourself and to others, and then to take action to rectify the problems that may have happened as a result of your past behaviors.

One thing that you will find when you take control over your life in this way is that the negative thought processes that you've had for so long simply vanish. Instead, you are going to be thinking in a more realistic and positive fashion that is going to involve making progress instead of wallowing the way that you have been with negative self-talk.

Chapter 7: Emotional Intelligence

Managing the self-talk that governs your life also involves managing your emotions. In turn, you are going to have to manage how you react to the emotions of others. Being skilled at doing so is often referred to as emotional intelligence. So, as we try to work our way out of a life governed by negative thoughts and self-talk, part of what we are doing is learning to develop our emotional intelligence.

Awareness

Emotional intelligence begins with an awareness of our own emotional states. This has to be clear and completely understood. One exercise that you can engage in is to go back and write down each instance where you have a thought of any kind. It can be negative self-talk or positive self-talk. Every time you have a thought that is worth writing down in your journal, also write down the emotional state that you're feeling at the time that you have the thought. See if you can recognize exactly what emotion it is. Sometimes the emotions will be simple and raw. You could be feeling depressed or melancholy, or maybe you feel angry. At other times the emotions might be a little more sophisticated, and in the beginning, it might be hard to identify them. So, you might feel angry, but what is really behind the anger? As an example, perhaps you are feeling a bit of resentment. In that case, rather than saying that it's anger, I would say that the true emotion is resentment.

You should also look to practice awareness when you're interacting with other people. Sometimes it's difficult to accurately estimate the emotions that other people are feeling. We are all bound to make mistakes when trying to interpret the feelings of others. Now, I'm not suggesting that you go out and actually confront people. Keep it to yourself. But try observing people—not just what they say or do, see if you can develop your emotional intelligence by becoming more aware of the emotional states that they may be experiencing.

In the last chapter, we mentioned that perhaps someone is having a bad day and it comes across that they don't like you. This is a skill that can become useful if you develop it over time. In other words, by closely observing people's emotions, it will help you to correctly interpret situations, rather than put it all as blame on you.

One way that you can do this, in the beginning, is to observe how some people are interacting with others casually. For example, your boss might come into your office and appear grouchy, and in the past, you would have interpreted this as either: "I did something wrong," or "My boss just doesn't like me." But with a little bit of heightened awareness, you might be paying attention to your boss as they interact with others in the office, and you might see that they have the same demeanor on that day with pretty much everyone they interact with. If that's the case, then you might use your emotional intelligence to try to understand what they are feeling and what their emotional state is. This has practical implications. When you're able to get a better sense of the emotional states that others are experiencing, you will be able to respond in a more appropriate manner. In all cases, taking an attitude of tolerance and understanding is going to be helpful. Again, that doesn't mean that you let yourself be abused. You use your judgment to determine when it's appropriate to be tolerant and when it's not.

Regulating Your Emotions

One of the aspects of emotional intelligence that is routinely considered is being able to regulate your own emotional states. This is very important when it comes to people who are suffering from negative programming, and who have been engaging in negative self-talk, possibly for decades. Learning to regulate your emotions is going to be one of the most important steps that you take.

When you have negative emotional states, many times, people simply experienced them without thinking about them. Start changing this by recognizing when you feel upset, depressed, frustrated, or angry. When you start to feel an emotional state, identify it in your mind. Say to yourself something to the effect of: "I am feeling frustrated right now." One of the things that this does is it helps to connect the left brain and the right brain together. Often the emotions we experience are felt through the right brain. Your language centers—and some people even suggest your consciousness (although nobody has proof about that really)—reside in your left brain. Emotions also rise from the nonverbal lower centers of the brain. That is why we feel emotions without always knowing how to vocalize about them. So, by making a statement about our emotional state, we help to involve the higher centers of our consciousness in the experience. This will help us to recognize our emotional states more clearly. And possibly more important, this is going to help us to manage them.

Frustration and anger are only useful if we recognize our emotional state and then do something about the cause of these feelings. Simply experiencing these emotions and fuming is not a sign of emotional intelligence. Instead, taking control of them and then turning them into positive self-talk is going to help you make actual progress in your life. Let's say that you get angry with your husband, who will not communicate when he is upset about something. Instead of just getting angry, you can recognize the emotional state and understand why you're feeling angry and frustrated. So, for example, you could then resolve to communicate in a loving and understanding way and explain to him that it would be helpful if he would explain how he is feeling and what is making him upset, rather than clamming up.

Becoming Sensitive to Emotional Signals

As you become more self-aware about your own emotional states and begin learning how to regulate them, you are also going to be able to develop more skills that will help you become sensitive to the emotional signals that others are giving off. In fact, this is something that you can start practicing right away. Again, I don't suggest confronting people, especially if it's not a personal relationship. Just make the observations and file them away in your own mind. But you can go beyond that. In other words, what you can do is start taking action based on the signals that you're getting from other people. This will help you learn and improve your emotional intelligence as well. There are going to be times when you make mistakes; however, you're going to find that you begin to find out when you are correct in your interpretation. So, this is a situation where you will learn as you go.

Changing Your Emotional States

Another aspect of emotional intelligence is learning how to alter your emotional state. This is actually easier than it sounds. Why is this important? This is actually totally relevant to the issue of negative self-talk. What happens with people who are prone to negative self-talk is they let themselves dwell in negative emotional states. Often you are not even fully aware of the emotional state that you are in. You might let it linger and gain more energy.

In any case, what is going to happen when you are letting yourself dwell in negative emotional states? Inevitably, you are going to start engaging in negative self-talk. You are already prone to this already, and so when you are feeling bad, the negative self-talk is going to come on and come on strongly.

This suggests learning to control your emotional states. We have already discussed the first step in this process, which is awareness. So, you need to recognize when you are in any given emotional state and tell yourself about it. "I am feeling really frustrated right now." Then work to replace the negative emotional state with a positive emotional state, or at least a neutral emotional state. One way to do this is to seek out an attitude of calm and peacefulness. Try breathing deeply and slowly. If you are able to, close your eyes as you breathe in and out, slowly. Don't think about anything. If you need to visualize something in order to keep your mind from engaging in negative self-talk, see yourself at the beach, or in an open field of flowers. Then, in your mind's ear, hear the sound of the waves lapping against the shore, or winds passing through some nearby trees. Keep breathing until you feel calm and relaxed.

If necessary, and if you have the ability to do so, go outside and take a quick five-minute walk. This can often help switch gears so that the negative emotional state that we have been experiencing gets replaced by more positive feelings.

You can also engage in positive affirmations when you recognize that you are feeling a negative emotional state. This can directly attack the tendency of your mind to bring out negative self-talk when you feel these types of emotional states.

Chapter 8: Strengthen the Mental Muscle

Now we've learned some ways that we can start transforming negative thoughts and emotions into positive ones. But remember that things are always going to get tough from time to time, and you are going to have to rely on yourself when times get difficult. You are your own best advocate and friend. Learn to rely on yourself first. This will help you get through tough situations, and it's also going to help you be a better partner, friend, and parent.

Get Tough and Have Your Own Back

If you have had negative self-talk throughout your life, then you are probably not a dominant person. And I am not going to suggest here that you become a dominant or controlling person, but what I am suggesting is that you learn to stand up for yourself. We all have our family, friends, and maybe you have a partner, but in the end, you have to stand up for yourself and not depend on others. Developing an ability to get tough in this manner is not just going to help you. It is also going to help you be a better person for others to have a relationship with, because they are going to be able to count on you when times get tough.

One of the first steps that you need to take when having your own back is not being afraid to speak out. Learn to speak out clearly and confidently and let people know that they cannot take you for granted. You should be able to express your needs clearly to other people and do it in a way that isn't hurtful.

Sometimes you are going to need to speak up. You might be treated unfairly at work, or you might get in a legal dispute with someone when you are in the right.

Don't be afraid to ask questions. Always make sure that people are communicating clearly and that you totally understand the situation. This is important in your personal and professional relationships. If you are having trouble with a manager at work, don't be afraid to take the initiative and go see them rather than wait for them to come and see you—or worse—they reprimand or fire you. Speak to them in a respectful but confident manner and ask questions. By asking questions, you can let your manager know that you are seeking to clarify the situation and get their expectations of you out in the open and crystal clear.

You should do the same when you are having conflicts in interpersonal relationships, and you don't know where the other person stands. You can take control by being the first person in the relationship to take action; you have your own back when you are the one to initiate communication and ask questions to get everything on the table.

Another aspect of having your own back is not relying strictly on what people say. Always verify what they claim in their speech by observing that they follow through with their actions. If someone owes you money, and they continually promise to pay you back, but they make no effort to do so, then you know this is a situation that you are going to need to take more seriously.

Boundaries are also important. All of us have some personal boundaries that we need to keep up, even with the people who are closest to us. If someone is violating what you feel are your personal boundaries, start by clearly explaining to that person what those personal boundaries are. If they continue to violate the boundaries after that, then you might reconsider your relationship with that person. If it's a family member, and you find that they are not respecting your personal boundaries even after you have clearly communicated them and what your expectations are, then you need to put some distance between yourself and that person until they make it clear that they are willing to respect the boundaries that you have set.

Remaining Strong in the Face of Adversity

As I said earlier, it is easy to write down thoughts in a book; it is hard to stay strong when times get tough. In order to remain strong, the first thing that you should do is adopt an attitude of calm acceptance. That doesn't mean that you're going to stay in a bad situation, rather, it means that you're going to be calm and peaceful and not get riled up with negative emotions that lead to panic and bring back the negative self-talk. From here, you should clearly work out the steps that you are going to take to change the situation. Use positive affirmations to give yourself the confidence to remain strong and positive. Keep asking questions—and look for the answers to develop steps to improve your situation.

Tips for Maintaining a Strong Mindset and Staying Positive

When faced with adversity, giving in to the same old negative thought processes is the easy way out, but it's also the natural inclination that you will have if you are coming from that place. Don't try to suppress your negative emotions—experience them as they are but use them to transform the situation. See a situation of adversity as a challenge, rather than viewing it as a negative. This will help you to start viewing life in an entirely different way. When facing a challenge, we try to work through it and get past it rather than giving in to it and feeling helpless. So, sit down and develop a plan to change the situation that is causing you adversity. Without a plan, the same problem is going to be there a week from now, a month from now, or a year from now. You are the one who has to take action to get out of the situation.

When faced with adversity, it is going to require you to call upon strength that you didn't realize you had. Break down the problem into small steps so that it's easier to force yourself to take the steps that are necessary in order to get out of it. Always use that approach when solving problems. View the problem, not as a whole, which is often overwhelming, but as smaller problems, each of which can be solved individually. Then start taking those small steps and making progress. You will find that you begin to develop a more positive attitude when using this type of approach, and you will also begin to feel better and gain confidence. Your emotional state will change from one that might be characterized as panic, to a serene calm, which gives you the confidence to push through.

Although it sounds strange, when you are feeling the most adversity, practice gratitude. Being thankful for the strength and abilities that you have will help you get through the most difficult times. There is no doubt that you have things to be thankful for, even in your darkest moments. By expressing gratitude, you are going to improve your mood and thought processes. This, in turn, is going to help you think more clearly and take a more positive attitude that is more conducive to solving your problems.

Also, focus on the positive. Remember filtering—there are always shades of gray in each situation that you encounter. Even if you are in an adverse situation where the negatives outweigh the positives—in the given moment—there are always positives to focus on and keep you upbeat.

Chapter 9: 500 Affirmations for a Positive and Optimistic Outlook

1. *I am unique, and my life has value.*
2. *I am confident.*
3. *I trust my own judgment.*
4. *I am optimistic and look forward to each day.*
5. *I am someone others can count on.*
6. *I choose to be successful.*
7. *I choose to be happy.*
8. *I love challenges; they bring out my strength.*
9. *I can create the life that I want.*
10. *I can draw on my own strength and power.*
11. *I believe in myself.*
12. *In the end, things work out for the best.*
13. *I accept myself for who I am.*
14. *It is human to make mistakes. I learn from my mistakes and move ahead stronger.*
15. *I feel good about being alive, and I enjoy my life.*
16. *Sometimes life is challenging, but it is also fun and rewarding.*
17. *Every problem presents an opportunity for growth.*

18. *I don't have to do anything; I choose to do things that work for me.*
19. *I can be counted on by others to meet any challenge.*
20. *I have the strength and stamina to get through anything.*
21. *I have compassion for myself and recognize that if I make a mistake it's not the end of the world.*
22. *I choose to be calm and peaceful.*
23. *I am successful.*
24. *With each passing day, I become more successful.*
25. *I can change the way I feel.*
26. *I recognize my strengths.*
27. *I attract people who are optimistic, happy, and positive.*
28. *I let go of negative thoughts and feelings.*
29. *I am honest and trustworthy.*
30. *I am capable of living a rich and full life.*
31. *I can have a fulfilling career.*
32. *My days are full of joy and laughter.*
33. *The number one emotion I feel is happiness.*
34. *I recognize the contributions of others but also of myself.*
35. *I will take credit when I deserve it.*
36. *I will not blame others for my mistakes but instead, take responsibility for them.*
37. *I make friends easily because I bring joy to people's lives.*
38. *I am pleasant to be around.*
39. *I am friendly and outgoing.*
40. *I have lots of energy and am passionate about everything that I do.*
41. *Amazing opportunities are there for me to take.*
42. *I will do what it takes to turn any wrong into a right.*
43. *I am not complacent; I have energy and enthusiasm for even the smallest task.*
44. *I have a lot to offer.*
45. *I can help people with my kindness and wisdom.*
46. *I look forward to meeting new people.*

47. *I find new situations and challenges exciting.*
48. *I have compassion and care for others with empathy and kindness.*
49. *I enjoy my work and consider no task to be beneath me.*
50. *I am smart and can tackle any problem.*
51. *I deserve love and happiness.*
52. *My thoughts and behavior are consistent.*
53. *I respect myself, and I respect others when they have earned it.*
54. *I deserve to be treated with respect and accept nothing less.*
55. *I am good to myself.*
56. *I know I can achieve anything I set my mind to.*
57. *Respecting myself first will help others respect me.*
58. *I like myself.*
59. *I can make my own decisions.*
60. *I have the power to create change.*
61. *I am happy with who I am, but I am willing to grow and change.*
62. *I let go of negative feelings about myself.*
63. *My self-discipline is growing stronger.*
64. *I am persistent and will work hard toward any goal.*
65. *I can choose any career path I want to.*
66. *I deserve to have a family that loves and respects me.*
67. *I am someone others can count on in a crisis.*
68. *I have the power to change myself.*
69. *I speak with clarity, confidence, and strength.*
70. *Other people value what I have to say.*
71. *My opinions matter.*
72. *If I have done my best, that is all I can do.*
73. *I have good self-esteem.*
74. *I love myself unconditionally.*
75. *I can heal myself.*
76. *I am willing and able to pay the price required to grow and become stronger.*

77. *If someone offers constructive criticism, it doesn't get me down.*
78. *Others respect me because I respect myself first.*
79. *Others love me because I love myself first.*
80. *Feeling confident comes naturally to me.*
81. *I can achieve anything and will do what it takes.*
82. *I have the power to change myself.*
83. *I do my best when meeting every challenge.*
84. *I have the power to change my situation.*
85. *I am flexible and open to change.*
86. *I forgive myself for making mistakes.*
87. *I can choose to live how I want to live.*
88. *I will not let others determine how I feel.*
89. *I choose to be happy no matter how bad things get.*
90. *Tomorrow is a new day with new opportunities.*
91. *I make mistakes, but everyone makes mistakes, and I learn from them.*
92. *I always look for the good in other people.*
93. *I am self-reliant and strong.*
94. *I am creative and see a way forward.*
95. *I attract positive and happy people.*
96. *I make other people happy because I am always striving to be happy and joyful.*
97. *I am eliminating negative energy from my life.*
98. *My talents make me unique.*
99. *I love and accept myself for who I am.*
100. *I am persistent and strive to look for solutions.*
101. *The universe fills me with joy and love.*
102. *People value my insight and knowledge.*
103. *I am always loved and respected.*
104. *I am not a prisoner of the past. I recognize mistakes I have made and learn from them, rather than dwelling on it.*
105. *I am full of courage and strength.*
106. *The universe is filling me with happiness, joy, and peace.*

Affirmations about Appearance

107. *I am not perfect, but nobody is.*
108. *I am beautiful and radiant.*
109. *Others see my beauty and are drawn to it.*
110. *I am always becoming more beautiful.*
111. *I accept who I am and appreciate my natural beauty.*
112. *I am attractive.*
113. *I am fit and healthy.*
114. *I am working to become even more fit, attractive, and healthy.*
115. *I take good care of my body.*
116. *I get the rest that my body needs and deserves.*
117. *I am losing weight and will lose weight as long as necessary.*
118. *My skin is smooth, radiant, and silky.*
119. *I have a wonderful smile.*
120. *I am not ashamed of my body.*
121. *My skin is unblemished.*
122. *I radiate an inner self-confidence, that enhances my natural beauty.*
123. *My hair is shiny, smooth, full, and beautiful.*
124. *I look great in pictures.*
125. *My smile makes others happy.*
126. *I attract people I want to attract.*
127. *Society cannot tell me what I am supposed to look like.*
128. *I will not give in to weight shaming; I lose weight to become healthier.*
129. *My body is beautiful.*
130. *I feel happy inside my body.*
131. *I feel healthy.*
132. *I will nourish my body with good and positive energy.*
133. *My happy and healthy attitude is making my body healthier every day.*
134. *I am sexy and desirable.*

135. *I nourish my body with the healthy foods and nutrients that it needs.*
136. *My teeth are white and beautiful.*
137. *My eyes sparkle when I smile.*
138. *My body is free of aches and pains.*
139. *My body is full of energy and can meet any challenge.*
140. *I am happy with my body the way it is.*
141. *I only eat when I am hungry.*
142. *When I am full, I stop eating.*
143. *I will do what's necessary to be healthy, but will not abuse my body.*
144. *My body is a temple, and I treat it as such.*
145. *If I am overweight, this has no impact on my worth or self-esteem.*
146. *If I am overweight, I will do what it takes to achieve optimal health.*
147. *Because I accept myself, I am comfortable in my own skin.*
148. *I dress appropriately for my body and look stylish and beautiful.*
149. *I am grateful for the food and nourishment the universe has provided me.*
150. *I am happy that I live in a world of plenty where I never want for food or nourishment.*
151. *I love exercising. It makes me feel great.*
152. *I am in control of my eating, and only eat as much as I need.*
153. *I am in control of my eating, and only eat foods that are healthy and nutritious.*
154. *I let go of any guilt I feel about food.*
155. *I am a real person and will not compare myself to Hollywood stars or models.*
156. *I am not embarrassed by my physical appearance.*
157. *I am attractive just the way I am.*
158. *I have a healthy relationship with food.*

159. *I can enjoy sweets and dessert once in a while without guilt or shame.*
160. *I am not ashamed of my body.*
161. *I will enjoy a life of health and longevity.*
162. *When I wake up in the morning, I feel strong, rested, and healthy.*
163. *My partner finds me attractive.*
164. *I am special.*
165. *My body does not define who I am.*
166. *I radiate inner and outer beauty.*
167. *My body image is not going to control my life.*
168. *I don't care what others think about my body or appearance.*
169. *I surround myself with love and acceptance.*
170. *I am secure in who I am, but always strive to improve.*
171. *I feel good about myself and my looks.*
172. *I do not need the validation of others for my appearance.*
173. *Nobody can reach perfection, but I can improve each day.*
174. *My kindness enhances my natural beauty.*
175. *My face is smooth and free of acne and blemishes.*
176. *I can feel my scars healing, and my skin becoming shiny and beautiful.*
177. *I look beautiful and also friendly; this makes it easy for others to approach me.*
178. *I feel good about the way I am without needing the validation of other people.*
179. *I do not compare myself to others. Everyone is unique and has their own values.*
180. *I seek to lose weight for my own health and well-being, not to please others.*
181. *Other people must accept me for who I am.*
182. *I cannot control what others think about my appearance.*

183. *I accept slow and steady progress when reaching my goals with exercise and healthy eating.*
184. *I enjoy eating a healthy diet.*
185. *I release all negative thoughts about my body.*
186. *I will not be shamed because of my appearance.*
187. *I can go in public without caring what others think about how I look.*
188. *I am OK if I eat an unhealthy meal or miss a day of exercise. We all deserve time to relax.*
189. *I eat to live and provide my body nourishment.*
190. *I do not feel guilty about eating.*
191. *I can control when I eat.*
192. *I feel great because I look great.*
193. *I look great no matter what I am wearing.*
194. *I feel great when I exercise and am full of strength and energy.*
195. *My strength and vitality grow every single day.*
196. *If I have a partner, they love me for who I am. My outer beauty is a bonus; it does not define me as a person.*
197. *I fill people's hearts with desire.*
198. *I am toned, fit, and strong.*
199. *I love the way I look when I see myself in the mirror.*
200. *I love how I look when I see myself in a photograph.*

Affirmations for Work and Career

201. *I work well under pressure.*
202. *I choose the kind of work I will do.*
203. *I have unlimited power to choose my career.*
204. *I am capable and will do what it takes to get ahead.*
205. *I have the knowledge necessary to make good decisions.*
206. *I make mistakes on the job, but I learn from them and do better next time.*
207. *People enjoy working with me and having me on their team.*
208. *I have the strength to overcome any obstacle.*
209. *I speak confidently at work.*

210. *I will be heard by my colleagues and supervisors.*
211. *I will not accept abuse and mistreatment at work.*
212. *My self-confidence is growing.*
213. *Today is going to be a great day at the office.*
214. *My colleagues at work love and respect me.*
215. *My opinion is valued by others.*
216. *My opinion is important.*
217. *I am intelligent and capable.*
218. *I can speak out with confidence, whether in a meeting or in private.*
219. *I am letting go of beliefs that restrict my success.*
220. *I deserve to get paid a fair wage for the work I do.*
221. *The world is full of unlimited opportunities.*
222. *I am capable of being my own boss.*
223. *I can start a business and become rich.*
224. *I set goals that I can meet.*
225. *My coworkers are supportive and friendly.*
226. *I have the power to attract wealth and prosperity.*
227. *I will let go of negative thoughts and emotions about others I work with.*
228. *I accept others for who they are and realize nobody is perfect.*
229. *I see the good in any situation at work.*
230. *I am smart enough to pursue any career that interests me.*
231. *I am focused on my goals and making progress.*
232. *I am always ready to accept new challenges.*
233. *I feel strong, confident, and able to meet any challenge I will face today.*
234. *I am enthusiastic about my work.*
235. *I will give my all to any task, no matter how small or trivial.*
236. *I will never stop growing.*
237. *During meetings, I feel strong and confident. My opinions matter.*

238. *Every day my confidence is increasing.*
239. *I am learning new things all the time and becoming more valuable to others.*
240. *I am grateful for the success I have achieved, and the coming years are only going to be better.*
241. *I am passionate about my work, and I look forward to each and every single day.*
242. *When I fail, it's a temporary setback, and I turn every failure into a success.*
243. *Failure is a learning opportunity.*
244. *I am surrounded by people who believe in me.*
245. *I look forward to going to work every single day.*
246. *I will push myself to become better.*
247. *I welcome any challenge and feel strong and confident.*
248. *The contributions I am making are powerful and valuable.*
249. *I am willing to work with anyone who respects me.*
250. *I deserve respect at work.*
251. *I am not afraid of change, and if I am not getting what I want at work, I will go elsewhere.*
252. *I have the confidence to change my situation if I need to.*
253. *I am growing all the time and becoming a better and stronger person.*
254. *I am free of self-doubt.*
255. *If I am disrespected, I have no fear of directly confronting it.*
256. *I am able to set goals at work and meet them in a timely fashion.*
257. *My potential for growth and achievement is limitless.*
258. *I succeed in everything that I do.*
259. *I am not afraid to strike out on my own.*
260. *I can succeed no matter what I do.*
261. *I am not afraid to pursue more education to make myself stronger and more useful to others.*

262. *I will mentor others who are like me, and teaching others makes me stronger.*
263. *I feel happy and free to make my own decisions.*
264. *I love my job but am not held prisoner by it.*

Affirmations for Wealth and Prosperity

265. *Wealth and prosperity flow to me daily.*
266. *I am able to manifest all the money that I need.*
267. *I am paying off all of my debts.*
268. *With each day that passes, I am becoming more financially secure.*
269. *The universe is full of wealth and abundance.*
270. *Money is never a problem for me.*
271. *I can make as much money as I need to be secure.*
272. *I feel good about money and prosperity.*
273. *Everyone deserves wealth, abundance, and prosperity.*
274. *Wealth and prosperity are flowing toward me.*
275. *I choose to be wealthy.*
276. *I enjoy my prosperity.*
277. *Being wealthy enables me to help others.*
278. *Making money is good for me, and helps me live independently.*
279. *I will not be a financial burden on others.*
280. *I am destined to make a lot of money.*
281. *Each year going forward, I will make more money than the last.*
282. *I always have enough money to meet my needs.*
283. *I always see new opportunities to make money.*
284. *My prosperity is always growing.*
285. *Wealth seems to find its way into my life.*
286. *My income is growing and will continue to grow.*
287. *I let go of a poverty mindset.*
288. *I am thankful for all the money I have received, and I look forward to receiving more money.*
289. *I love money and love sharing it with others.*
290. *Sharing my prosperity is a gift, not a burden.*

291. *I am gaining wealth through honest work.*
292. *I deserve to be wealthy, healthy, and prosperous.*
293. *I deserve my success.*
294. *I am a wealthy person.*
295. *I can create as much wealth as I want.*
296. *The world is full of opportunities to make money.*
297. *Wealth is a gift from the universe, and we all deserve it. But it is up to me to seize it.*
298. *Money makes me feel joyful, but my life does not revolve around money.*
299. *Money is good because it allows me to take care of myself and my family.*
300. *Every single day brings new opportunities to make money.*
301. *I am suddenly seeing new ways to make more money.*
302. *If I am not wealthy, I cannot help others.*
303. *The universe provides me with enough money to meet my needs.*
304. *There is wealth all around us; we only need to look for it.*
305. *I choose to think in terms of prosperity and wealth.*
306. *I let go of all the negative feelings I've had about money.*
307. *I am successful and prosperous.*
308. *I deserve to make a lot of money for what I do for others.*
309. *Prosperity flows to me without resistance.*
310. *I freely attract money and wealth.*
311. *I love money, but it's not the only good thing in my life.*
312. *I share money with others freely, because I know there are unlimited amounts of it.*
313. *I find it easy to make any amount of money.*
314. *I think in terms of prosperity and abundance.*
315. *I feel abundance all around me.*
316. *I attract others who can make money.*

317. *I am always thinking of new ways to make money and freely share my ideas with others.*
318. *I feel happy and joyful, and this attracts wealth, prosperity, and abundance.*
319. *Money is my birthright.*
320. *I deserve abundance and happiness.*
321. *I have the power to be successful and make any amount of money I choose.*
322. *I feel relaxed around money.*
323. *My debts are evaporating and being replaced by prosperity.*
324. *I can manage my finances with skill and confidence.*
325. *The amount of wealth in the universe is unlimited.*
326. *I do not feel guilty about my desire to be wealthy.*
327. *Wealth is not a matter of luck; I create wealth by applying the power of my mind.*
328. *When I create a business, it attracts customers eager to give me their money.*
329. *My customers give me their money because I provide them value in return.*
330. *The value I provide for others is worth unlimited amounts of money.*
331. *I can achieve any level of success.*
332. *I am extremely powerful and capable of earning money.*
333. *My financial situation improves with each passing day.*
334. *If I am not happy with my job, I am confident enough to find a new one that pays more money.*
335. *Each day, I feel more comfortable around money.*
336. *I am constantly attracting money into my life.*
337. *I am constantly attracting financial opportunities into my life.*
338. *People who can make money are attracted to me.*
339. *I will partner with others to make money, but I can take care of myself.*

340. *I do not need anyone to make enough money to take care of me, as I can support myself financially.*
341. *I find making money fun and enjoyable.*
342. *I feel confident that the universe will bring me all the money, wealth, and abundance that I could ever need.*
343. *My basic needs—food, shelter, and security—are always satisfied because I have enough money.*
344. *I have no problems accessing credit.*
345. *I have good credit, and it is always improving.*
346. *I feel comfortable being wealthy and having a lot of money.*
347. *I deserve to have more money than I ever dreamed of.*
348. *Poverty is evil; being rich is good.*
349. *I reject self-limiting beliefs that trap people in poverty or struggle.*
350. *I am smart enough to learn about business and finances.*
351. *I am a skilled investor who always seems to make money.*
352. *I can make money no matter how the economy is doing.*
353. *When I encounter struggles making money, I can come up with new plans to make new money.*
354. *There is always money to be made, and I will make it.*
355. *Everyone deserves to make money, but it is up to each of us to seek it out.*
356. *I will live a good and positive life, no matter how much money I make.*
357. *I will help others with my money, but won't sacrifice my wants and needs to do so.*
358. *If I am in a difficult situation, I will change it so that I can make more money.*
359. *The fact that others have made money proves I can make money too.*
360. *There are no limits to my financial success.*
361. *The more money I make, the more abundance flows to me.*

362. *My thoughts seem to attract money and wealth.*
363. *My bank account and stocks are constantly growing in value.*
364. *I never have problems paying any bills.*

Affirmations for Health and Safety

365. *I feel healthy and strong.*
366. *Every day, I feel youthful and vigorous.*
367. *I recover from illnesses easily.*
368. *I don't get sick often.*
369. *My body and immune system are strong.*
370. *I provide my body with the rest it needs to be healthy and strong.*
371. *I provide my body with the nutrients it needs for health.*
372. *I will live a long and prosperous life.*
373. *My body is free from disease and sickness.*
374. *Every day I become stronger.*
375. *My energy always seems to be increasing.*
376. *I feel younger than I did twenty years ago.*
377. *I will not abuse my body with alcohol or drugs.*
378. *I only eat healthy foods.*
379. *I enjoy exercise and the feelings of strength and health that it brings.*
380. *I will live a long time and will be free of disease.*
381. *My body is freeing itself from disease and disability.*
382. *I no longer feel any pain.*
383. *I am strong and flexible.*
384. *I can defeat cancer, heart disease, and diabetes.*
385. *I never seem to get sick, even when others around me are getting illnesses.*
386. *I deserve to be completely free from illness.*
387. *I am free from back and joint pain.*
388. *I will not suffer from arthritis.*
389. *Every cell in my body is full of loving energy and is healthy.*
390. *If I am sick, I will return to health with time.*

391. I will not let my mind get in the way of healing.
392. My body is grateful for the way I am taking care of it.
393. I am improving my health daily.
394. I enjoy the food that keeps my body healthy.
395. I live a life of balance, and this improves my health.
396. I am thankful for the health that I have enjoyed.
397. I am grateful for the gift of my life and pledge to live it to the fullest from this day forward.
398. I will seek out help with my health when I need it.
399. I respect my body and treat it with the respect it deserves.
400. I accept natural healing and welcome its power.
401. I deserve good health, and I claim it as my divine right.
402. Every day I am getting healthier.
403. I can enjoy junk food without guilt, but only in moderation.
404. I am in possession of a healthy mind.
405. I reject unnecessary worry about health. I will not be a hypochondriac.
406. I am safe.
407. I feel safe in my home.
408. I live in a good and safe neighborhood.
409. I deserve to be safe and protected.
410. I deserve safety and claim it as my divine right.
411. I trust my intuition and will listen to it if it warns me about my safety.
412. I feel safe wherever I go.
413. The universe protects me anywhere and at any time.
414. I am safe in this world.
415. I feel safe no matter where I go. It feels like someone is watching out for me.
416. I have everything I need to be safe and secure.
417. I have friends and family I can depend on for safety.
418. The world is full of kindness.
419. I have the power to create my own safety and security.

420. My loved ones are always safe and secure.
421. My children are safe and protected.
422. My body is safe and without risk.
423. I am safe at all times.
424. I feel secure when I travel.
425. I am always protected.
426. Everyone I love is safe and secure.
427. I am free from accidents and danger on the road.
428. I am always safe when I fly on an airplane.
429. My home is a haven of safety, protected from everything in this world.
430. I am safe and protected by the universal good. My world is surrounded by kindness and joy.
431. I am confident in my ability to protect myself and those around me.
432. My body is safe, secure, and protected.
433. I choose to feel safe and secure.
434. I feel safe and protected at all times.
435. I feel protected by the kindly divine spirit.
436. My intuition warns me of any potential danger.
437. I see myself traveling home at night in safety and security.
438. My world is a safe world.
439. My family is always safe.
440. I will take action to enhance the safety and security of my home.

Affirmations for Love and Romance

441. I deserve a loving relationship.
442. I deserve the respect of my partner.
443. I will only stay in a relationship based on loving kindness and respect.
444. I refuse to be abused or taken advantage of.
445. I will make my needs and feelings known to my partner.
446. I am confident about expressing my needs.

447. I love, admire, and respect my partner, and expect love, admiration, and respect in return.
448. I have unconditional love for my partner.
449. I deserve unconditional love.
450. I accept my partner for who they are, and expect them to accept me for who I am.
451. I expect my personal boundaries to be respected.
452. I will not stay in a relationship that is physically or emotionally abusive.
453. I am strong and confident and deserve unconditional love and respect.
454. I will respect the personal boundaries of others.
455. I will not force my partner to change and accept them for who they are.
456. I will not judge the people in my life, and they will not judge me.
457. I enjoy spending time with the people that I love.
458. I feel fulfillment in my relationships.
459. I am in a relationship where I am constantly growing and becoming whole.
460. I show my loved ones, including my partner, that I care about them.
461. I love unconditionally even though the people around me might not always treat me with respect.
462. I will show my loved ones how much I care for them.
463. I attract loving people into my life.
464. I am not afraid of change and will change my relationships if necessary.
465. I am able to communicate openly and honestly with my partner, friends, and family.
466. I am confident enough to communicate with complete honesty.
467. I do my best not to hurt the feelings of others in my life.
468. I do not fear emotional intimacy—I embrace it.
469. I welcome the love that the universe brings me.

470. I feel joy and loved when around my partner.
471. I am letting go of anger and negative feelings when thinking about my partner.
472. I reject feelings of jealousy and resentment.
473. I feel a sense of contentment when surrounded by the people I love.
474. My partner makes me feel safe and secure.
475. If I don't have a partner, it is only a matter of time before I find the perfect mate.
476. There is love and joy throughout the universe, and I will find someone to share it with.
477. I have unlimited love to give and share with others.
478. I love my family and accept them unconditionally.
479. I will share unconditional love with a partner.
480. When I get in petty disputes with loved ones, I forgive and forget and move on.
481. I will take responsibility when I hurt other people's feelings.
482. When I have injured another person emotionally, I will heal them.
483. While I will freely give of myself, I will expect to be paid back in like with kindness, love, and joy.
484. I deserve healthy and happy relationships.
485. I deserve unconditional love.
486. I deserve to have my own family.
487. I deserve love and respect.
488. My family provides love, care, and security.
489. I experience joy when I see my loved ones.
490. I know that my partner has my back at all times.
491. I am strong enough to provide complete support for my partner.
492. I enjoy celebrations with my family members.
493. I enjoy getting together with friends.
494. My friends can count on me, and I can count on them.

495. I have many friends who will provide support when I need it.

496. I am strong and able to give my friends support when they need me.

497. Life is full of joy, friendship, and love.

498. I look forward to each day, and the joy and love I will experience.

499. I am a wonderful and supportive parent and support my children with unconditional love.

500. I am strong, capable, kind, and loving, and would make a perfect partner for anyone.

Conclusion

Thank you for taking the time to read *Self Talk: The Ultimate Guide to Transforming Negative Thinking into Positive Thinking and Skyrocketing Self-Esteem, Confidence, Productivity, and Mental Toughness, Including 500 Daily Affirmations.*

I truly hope that you have found this book to be helpful and that you will find it useful in going forward. If you have enjoyed the book and found it to be educational, please leave a review on Amazon, I would much appreciate it.

The words that we say inside our heads throughout the day, every single day, have a large influence over how we feel about ourselves. The types of thoughts echoed by our inner voice are effectively running on autopilot, and are guided by programs that have wired our mind to think with certain negative patterns. The groundwork for these programs was laid down long ago, starting in childhood. It may seem that it is impossible to overcome them; however, we can learn to reprogram our "autopilot" and replace the negative self-talk we hear every day with positive thoughts and feelings. These, in turn, will lead to better and healthier results throughout our entire lives.

I hope that the methods discussed in this book will help you and that you will have stories of a positive transformation to share. I look forward to hearing them and will enjoy reading about them.

Thank you again for taking the time to read this book! May your life be filled with many happy and joyous days in the years ahead.

Check out another book by Mark Dudley

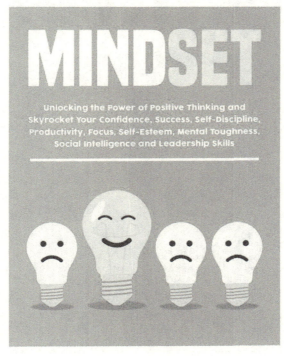

You might like this one as well

Made in the USA
Coppell, TX
11 September 2022